The Modern Poster

THE MODERN POSTER

STUART WREDE

THE MUSEUM OF MODERN ART, NEW YORK

DISTRIBUTED BY NEW YORK GRAPHIC SOCIETY BOOKS / LITTLE, BROWN AND COMPANY, BOSTON

This publication has been made possible by a generous grant from The May Department Stores Company

The exhibition *The Modern Poster* has been sponsored by The May Department Stores Company and the National Endowment for the Arts

Published on the occasion of the exhibition *The Modern Poster,* June 6–September 6, 1988, organized by Stuart Wrede, Director, Department of Architecture and Design, The Museum of Modern Art, New York

The color plates in this volume were photographed by Kate Keller, Chief Fine Arts Photographer, The Museum of Modern Art, and Mali Olatunji, Fine Arts Photographer, The Museum of Modern Art, with the exception of plates 214, 162, and 169 by David Allison, New York.
The black-and-white illustrations are credited to the following photographers and sources by figure number: Courtesy Lucy Broido, 3; Courtesy Elaine Lustig Cohen, 37; Rita Fernandez, 1, 4, 5, 6, 9, 11, 12, 13, 16, 17, 18, 19, 20, 22, 25, 26, 27, 28, 29, 31, 32, 36; Kate Keller, 21; The Library of Congress, 2; James Mathews, 8, 10, 35; André Morain, 34; Rolf Petersen, 24; The Pierpont Morgan Library, 7.

Edited by Harriet Schoenholz Bee
Designed by Steven Schoenfelder
Production by Tim McDonough
Typeset by Trufont Typographers Inc., Hicksville, N.Y.
Color separations by Reprocolor Llovet, Barcelona
Printed and bound by Cayfosa, Barcelona
Distributed outside the United States and Canada by Thames and Hudson Ltd., London

The Museum of Modern Art
11 West 53 Street
New York, New York 10019

Printed in Spain

CONTENTS

FOREWORD

This book is published in conjunction with the exhibition *The Modern Poster*, a comprehensive selection from the Museum's extensive poster collection. It is the first such presentation since the exhibition *Word and Image* of 1968. Since that time, the graphic design collection has more than doubled in size, reflecting the continuing addition of both contemporary work and classic examples of earlier decades.

We are profoundly grateful to all the designers and many friends of the Museum who have given generously to the collection. We owe a special debt of gratitude to the poster collection's most devoted supporter, Leonard A. Lauder, whose thoughtfulness and connoisseurship have enriched it immeasurably.

This exhibition and its accompanying publication would not have been possible without a major grant from The May Department Stores Company, for which we are deeply appreciative. Their support admirably reflects a continuing commitment in their own programs to high standards of graphic design. Additional support was provided by the National Endowment for the Arts, for which we are also most grateful.

Finally, we owe our thanks to the director of the exhibition and author of this volume, Stuart Wrede. The task of selecting some three hundred images from more than four thousand to exemplify the development of the modern poster requires a good eye and discriminating judgment. He has very admirably applied these qualities both to this book and to the exhibition it accompanies.

Richard E. Oldenburg
Director
The Museum of Modern Art

PREFACE AND ACKNOWLEDGMENTS

It is now twenty years since the exhibition *Word and Image*, the first comprehensive presentation of The Museum of Modern Art's extensive poster collection, was organized by Mildred Constantine. The accompanying catalogue, with an essay by Alan M. Fern, did much to define the history of the medium and its important landmarks, and is now an acknowledged classic in the field. Since 1968, the Museum's collection has grown from two thousand to over four thousand posters, as works of the intervening years were acquired, and equally important, gaps in the Museum's collection of posters from earlier periods were filled. A new exhibition and book appeared to be more than warranted.

This volume, however, does not aspire to be a comprehensive historical survey but, rather, is an effort to present the finest examples of the art of the poster created during the medium's approximately one hundred years of existence. I am, of course, only too aware of the gaps still present in the Museum's own collection as well as of the vast amount of excellent work that I have not been able to include.

For assistance in the preparation of the exhibition *The Modern Poster* and its accompanying publication I owe a major debt to Robert Coates, Study Center Supervisor in the Department of Architecture and Design, whose dedication to and knowledge of the Museum's poster collection has been invaluable. He has been a close collaborator on all aspects of the exhibition, and his expertise has been essential to its success. In the Department of Architecture and Design I am also grateful to Matilda McQuaid for her careful research on many of the posters and their designers, and for securing photographs for the publication. I am equally grateful to Christopher Mount for his help with research and his assistance throughout the preparation of the exhibition, and to Marie-Anne Evans for her assistance in all aspects of this project.

The organization of a large exhibition requires the collaboration of many members of the Museum's staff. Special thanks go to Richard E. Oldenburg, Director of the Museum, for his support throughout the planning of this project. I am grateful for the enthusiasm and expertise of Sue B. Dorn, Deputy Director for Development and Public Affairs, and Lacy Doyle, Development Manager, in securing support for the exhibition. James Snyder, Deputy Director for Planning and Program Support, and Richard Palmer, Coordinator of Exhibitions, have lent their valuable expertise on budgeting and scheduling. Jerome Neuner, Production Manager, has once again, with his skilled staff, built a finely crafted exhibition installation. Fred Coxen has done a masterful job of supervising the framing of the large number of posters for the exhibition. I am most grateful to Antoinette King and her staff in the Department of Conservation, particularly Karl Buchberg, Reba Fishman, and Harriet Stratis, for their expert restoration work. I am also appreciative of the work of other colleagues at the Museum for their invaluable contributions to the success of this endeavor in various areas: Priscilla Barker, Louise Chinn, Jeanne Collins, Emily Kies, and Jessica Schwartz.

I am also grateful to a number of friends, colleagues, and associates outside the Museum with whom I have discussed the exhibition and who have made many valuable suggestions. These include Jack Banning, Robert Brown, Ivan Chermayeff, Elaine Lustig Cohen, Mildred Constantine, James Fraser, Keith Godard, Caroline Hightower, Leonard A. Lauder, and Susan Reinhold.

I owe a special debt of gratitude to the members of the Department of Publications and their associates for the success of this volume. I particularly wish to thank Harriet Schoenholz Bee, Managing Editor, who has done an invaluable job editing the manuscript with her usual skill, humor, and dedication. It has been a great pleasure as well to work with Steven Schoenfelder, whose elegant design reinforces the quality of the material included in the publication. Tim McDonough, Production Manager, has with his usual expert eye supervised the production and printing of the book, whose superb quality owes much to his efforts. I also thank William P.

Edwards, Deputy Director of Auxiliary Services, for his enthusiasm for the project, and Nancy T. Kranz, Manager of Promotion and Special Services, for her efforts in promoting the book.

To my colleague John Elderfield, Director of the Department of Drawings, go my grateful thanks for reading the manuscript and offering valuable suggestions and comments. Special thanks are due Richard Tooke, Supervisor of Rights and Reproductions; Kate Keller, Chief Fine Arts Photographer; and Mali Olatunji, Fine Arts Photographer, for the photography of over three hundred posters in color. I am most grateful to James Fraser, Director of the Library, Fairleigh Dickinson University, Madison Campus, and his staff for bringing their expertise to the task of producing a bibliography for this book; I must take responsibility for any of its shortcomings, as copyfitting exigencies dictated limitations in the number of entries. My thanks go to Ex Libris for the loan of the avant-garde publication *De Stijl*. Others who have helped in various ways whom I particularly wish to acknowledge are Magdalena Dabrowski, Janis Ekdahl, Peter Galassi, Marisa Hill, Clive Phillpot, Rona Roob, Barbara Ross, Alarik Skarstrom, Daniel Starr, Kristin Teegarden, and Maura Walsh.

This endeavor would not have been possible without the kind support of numerous designers and friends of the Department of Architecture and Design who have generously donated posters or funds to purchase posters for the collection over the years. To all of them I owe particular thanks. I would like once again to express the Museum's and my own gratitude to Leonard A. Lauder, whose enthusiastic support has been critical in expanding and rounding out the collection. I would also like to express my own thanks to David C. Farrell and The May Department Stores Company for their generosity, which has been crucial for both the exhibition and the publication.

Finally, I wish to acknowledge my deep gratitude to Arthur Drexler for encouraging me to take on this project. During his thirty years as Director of the Department of Architecture and Design, the Museum's poster collection achieved its present range and quality.

Stuart Wrede
Director
Department of Architecture and Design

THE MODERN POSTER

"Catalogues, posters, advertisements of all sorts.
Believe me, they contain the poetry of our epoch."
—Guillaume Apollinaire, 1912[1]

Although posters were not formally acquired by The Museum of Modern Art until 1935,[2] its first director, Alfred H. Barr, Jr., had the medium in mind from the beginning. In 1929, the year of its inauguration, he proposed that the new museum "would probably expand beyond the narrow limits of painting and sculpture in order to include departments devoted to drawings, prints, and photography, typography, the arts of commerce and industry, architecture, stage designing, furniture, and the decorative arts."[3]

Today the broad range of the Museum's program is taken for granted. Its success tends to obscure the unique characteristics of the period in which the Museum was founded when a reevaluation of Western artistic sensibilities was taking place in all the arts. Not only was the new art seen as inseparable from the social and industrial changes of the day, but there was an unprecedented cross-fertilization among the various mediums.

Initially, social and industrial changes in the nineteenth century had elicited very different reactions from architects and designers, and from artists. Reformers in architecture and the applied arts were the first to try to come to terms with the social, cultural, and formal issues raised by industrialization. They sought to impose order on the ensuing chaos—on its artifacts (including graphics) and on its urban growth. Artists, in contrast, at first ignored these issues and took an art-for-art's-sake position. But then, in the first years of the twentieth century, it was they who derived a new aesthetic from the apparent chaos of the new industrial and urban environment. The evolution of these contradictory efforts and their subsequent convergence in the 1920s set the stage for a modernist synthesis of the arts that, among other things, inspired the multifaceted outlook of the Museum's program, with the poster an integral part of it.

The industrial revolution, by shattering familiar patterns of manufacture, generating new artifacts, and making others obsolete, forced fundamental reassessments for design. The advent of new inventions and techniques for production raised the question of the appropriate forms for these new objects. A dichotomy developed between a utilitarian approach and one that sought to impose traditional decorative forms on the new artifacts. In fact, one might view the evolution of modern design as the attempt to reconcile the rupture between function and manufacturing technique, on the one hand, and form, on the other, caused by industrialization.

The medium of print—or typography—in books, journals, newspapers, posters, broadsides, and advertising was one genre of artifact that proliferated, as the principal means of creating markets for the new products.

The lack of visual standards was put into perspective by the increased knowledge of cultures of the past; cultural anthropology and art history became firmly established disciplines at this time. Civilizations came to be judged by the artifacts they produced, and the inchoate products of the new industrial culture were compared unfavorably with the coherent artifacts of past cultures.

In England, the founding of the Museum of Ornamental Art, later the Victoria and Albert—the first museum devoted to the applied and decorative arts—in 1852 and the Arts and Crafts movement in 1859 reflected contemporary concern over the lack of stylistic coherence. William Morris's Arts and Crafts movement sought to revive interest in the crafts and improve the everyday artifacts of the masses. It evinced strong social concerns about the alienation of the industrial labor force, but its proposals looked to the past, to the Gothic style as an aesthetic model, and to the abolition of industrialization and a return to craft guilds. Moreover, its ideals came to be seen as unrealistic because, among other reasons, they tended to result in artifacts only the wealthy could afford.

Subsequent reformers, while recognizing the inevitability of industrialization looked to other sources for a model. The Belgian artist Henry van de Velde, one of the creators and the chief theorist of Art Nouveau, looked to the forms of nature.

Many of the designers of the Deutscher Werkbund, a highly influential organization founded in 1907 that sought to raise design standards and bring designers and industry together, looked to a simplified classicism for a new order. Only tentatively did they look to the machine itself. The social and theoretical ideas of these designers stressed a new unified aesthetics which would embrace architecture, the applied arts, and graphics, and reflect modern culture and means of production. Their ideas, more than their designs, were to be a fundamental contribution to subsequent development.

For artists and poets the problem was quite different. The Western countries had been radically transformed by the industrial revolution, but they had remained firmly wedded to traditional cultural forms in the arts. By the end of the nineteenth century the discrepancy between the forms of traditional culture and everyday life became increasingly apparent: art was not drawing its energy and inspiration from its own epoch.

Rapid industrialization had fostered the chaotic growth of the big city. The reality of this new urban environment was constant transformation and random juxtaposition of scale and diverse elements. To the average eye, accustomed to a traditional, harmonious sense of beauty, the new city must have appeared an alienating environment. However, to avant-garde poets and artists it was a realm from which they extracted a new aesthetic, much as artists of the seventeenth century had found an order in the natural landscape, which not so long before had appeared threatening and chaotic. In that context, one important aspect of modern art in its many manifestations is the "found" aesthetic of the big city.

The development of a new way of seeing that cultivated the unexpected, chance juxtaposition of images, the viewing of objects out of their familiar contexts, and the layering of disparate images was fundamental to the new aesthetic of the first decades of the twentieth century. The ubiquitous poster hoardings themselves were assemblages of diverse images (figure 1). While many were neatly tended, others consisted of a mixture of old posters partly torn off with new ones pasted over them. This urban environment undoubtedly contributed to the "collage" aesthetic first developed by the Cubists.

While the radical transformation in art first evolved in Paris in the work of individual artists, it was soon appropriated and transformed by a number of avant-garde groups. Prototypical were the Futurists, who sought to expand their activities to all artistic mediums and all aspects of everyday life, including politics. Characteristic of those movements formed before and during the war—Futurism and Dada—was a strong destructive and subversive element. In the first *Manifesto of Futurism* of 1909, the movement's leader Filippo Tommaso Marinetti declared, "We will bring down the museums, libraries, academies of every kind."[4] The Futurists exulted in disruptive tactics and saw war as the hygiene of the world.[5] The Dadaists took a more subversive approach. Ostensibly against art, Dada sought to undermine it by elevating chance and nonsense as cultural icons. Both movements, having literary origins, also focused considerable energy on revolutionizing typography.

In contrast to Futurism and Dada, whose activities were directed, as often as not, toward the demise of traditional cultural forms, the principal avant-garde movements formed after the war—de Stijl, Constructivism, and Purism—concentrated on building a new order. While rejecting Futurism's anarchic side, the more sober but utopian postwar avant-garde groups embraced its enthusiasm for the machine and the new industrial city. They did not turn against the machine, although it had provided the vast mechanical, destructive power of the war, but against the individualism, emotionalism, and romanticism they felt had caused it.

The Dutch artists of de Stijl sought to unite architecture, painting, typography, and design into an abstract, geometric unity that would harmonize existence. Their impetus came from the painter Piet Mondrian, who had evolved his own rectilinear, asymmetrical, geometric abstractions from Cubism. In Russia, Constructivism and Suprematism, also influenced by Cubism, provided fundamental formal stimuli for architecture, the applied arts, and typography during the 1920s.

In Paris, Purist painting sought to synthesize the formal innovations of Cubism with the harmony and order of the French classical tradition. Its founders, Charles-Édouard Jeanneret (better known as Le Corbusier) and Amédée Ozenfant, also edited the influential magazine *L'Esprit Nouveau*, through which they sought to show how developments in engineering, industry, and science were radically changing the conditions of life and forming the new culture.

The new abstract aesthetic that evolved in various forms among the avant-garde art groups in the 1920s coincided with the aspirations of progressive designers in architecture and the applied arts (some of whom were members of the groups), and provided them with a new formal language that they had only, in isolated examples, reached on their own.

The Bauhaus played the culminating and perhaps most visible role in the 1920s in the effort to consolidate all the arts of the modern period. Underlying the Bauhaus idea was a cultural and educational agenda that sought to combine the radical, new abstract formal language of the various avant-garde movements with architecture, the applied arts, and industry to make it an integral part of everyday life. Under the school's first director, architect Walter Gropius, the Bauhaus brought together the leading artists and designers of the day. Its unique program carried the Deutscher Werkbund's idea of unifying art and industry a crucial step further—to the radical formal innovations in art as the new source of inspiration. The Bauhaus was of fundamental importance for Barr in establishing the program of The Museum of Modern Art.

It was no coincidence that the avant-garde art movements had included architects and designers, and had tried to expand their newfound visual language among the various fine and applied artistic mediums, nor that these goals had agreed with the aspirations of the reformers in the applied arts. A basic impulse had come from the discipline of art history, which sought to document the coherence of the various arts, fine and applied, of any given period. It made artists, architects, designers, critics, and theoreticians of the art of the contemporary era aware of the historical imperative for what was clearly a new epoch. In this sense, Barr's studies at Princeton, which stressed the interrelatedness of all the arts, were just as fundamental for his conception of the Museum.[6]

The poster, a medium of its time, has always existed at the junction of the fine and applied arts, culture and commerce. As a hybrid medium it has provided an arena where painting, drawing, photography, and typography came together in new ways, influencing each other in the process. Its approximately one-hundred-year history coincides with that of modern art itself. Thus, it is not surprising that the poster fascinated Barr and became an integral part of the Museum's collection. The following discussion will focus on the evolution of the poster itself as a medium of expression and on its relationship with the other arts represented in the Museum.

Figure 1. Typical poster hoarding, Metropole Hotel Building, New York, 1909. Bettmann Archive, New York

Lithography was invented by Aloys Senefelder in 1796, but it was not until the latter part of the nineteenth century that the art of the poster can be said to have begun. Jules Chéret is generally credited with initiating its development and popularization. Aided by technical advances in color lithography, which he studied in England where he also saw large, American woodcut circus posters (figure 2), Chéret returned to Paris and gradually changed the medium. Small letterpress posters and handbills, sometimes with accompanying woodcut images, had dominated the streets. Chéret's early posters, such as *Le Chateau a Toto* of 1868 (figure 3), were a novelty in Paris, although they resemble Victorian illustration. However, it is the evolution of his style during the final decades of the nineteenth century, from *Les Girard* (plate 1) to the proto-Art Nouveau *Folies-Bergère, La Loïe Fuller* (plate 2), and his technical inventiveness that place Chéret in a preeminent position in the early emergence of the poster form. Nevertheless, despite his important influence on subsequent designers, Chéret remained tied to the nineteenth-century tradition of popular illustration, which he combined with inspiration drawn from great artists of the past such as Giovanni Battista Tiepolo and Jean Antoine Watteau.

The influence of Japanese prints (figure 4) was decisive on the subsequent development of the poster. In 1867, when the shogunate—which had isolated Japan for two centuries—fell, Japan took a pavilion at the Universal Exposition in Paris. The exposition provided the first opportunity for the Parisian public to view Japanese art. Nevertheless, Édouard Manet's small lithographic poster *Champfleury–Les Chats*, done the following year and clearly inspired by Japanese prints (figures 5, 6), remained an isolated example for some time. But by 1890 the influence of Japan on the Post-Impressionist painters was pervasive, as can be seen in the pioneering posters of Pierre Bonnard and Henri de Toulouse-Lautrec, among other art of the period. Bonnard's first poster, *France-Champagne* of 1891 (plate 6), prompted Toulouse-Lautrec to learn the art himself. What is remarkable about the work of both artists is the way they appropriated essential formal devices of Japanese prints—flat color surfaces, asymmetrical cropped compositions, and flowing outlines—but transformed them into art very much their own and of their time.

While the frivolity of Bonnard's *France-Champagne* poster is in the spirit of Chéret, there is a wit to Toulouse-Lautrec's renderings (plates 3–5) that owes much to the French caricature tradition of Honoré Daumier. These street-smart images, rendered with an economy of means, were peculiarly suited to the art of the poster. It is not surprising that Toulouse-Lautrec's art tends to be associated with the poster medium. In his work, in addition to the broad outlines of the figures, the diagonal—a Japanese device to suggest depth and to animate the composition—becomes an important element.

In contrast, Bonnard's subsequent posters, *Les Peintres Graveurs* and *La Revue Blanche* (plates 7, 8), develop further in the direction of abstraction and flatness. Working in both with a light and dark color field and a highly ambiguous figure-ground relationship, Bonnard, through subtle abstracted gestures, draws out the figures from the flat color field. While *La Revue Blanche* is the more successful composition, *Les Peintres Graveurs* is fascinating both for the roughly rendered letters and for their positive-negative transformation as they cross from one field to the other.

The posters of Alphonse Mucha have come to be seen as the essence of Art Nouveau. If there was still a naive gaiety and optimism in the work of Chéret, a sense of joy and even innocence in his animated women, there is a languorous, world-weary sophistication in the women that dominate the posters of Mucha (plates 9, 10). Their animated, serpentine locks of hair (drawn with lines that are both outline and shadow) have some of the intricacy and richness of Celtic ornament, which also inspired other designers of the period.

The purpose of many early posters was to advertise entertainment. In capturing the spirit of places or events they are extraordinary documents of popular culture. They also quickly came to be collected and displayed for their own sakes, poster exhibitions were organized, and books devoted to posters were published. The first exhibition devoted exclusively to posters was held in Paris in 1884. Journals appeared in Paris in 1897 and in London in 1898, essentially aimed at poster collectors. This interest reached Germany later and coincided with its subsequent preeminence in poster design.

Although posters influenced the avant-garde, they were not at the forefront of formal innovation in the arts. Their significance lay in the fact that they conveyed the vitality of the popular culture and in their mechanical reproducibility. They were also accessible to the populace, had an impact on the urban streetscape, promoted products, and were easily affordable or free. In its early years the poster reflected bourgeois amusements, and was often of dubious artistic merit. Its potential for treating serious issues was not yet recognized.

A significant, early exception was Carlos Schwabe's poster of 1892 for the first Salon Rose + Croix exhibition (plate 27). The purpose of the poster was not only to advertise the exhibition but also to embody in allegorical form the philosophy of redemption through art, the goal of this esoteric, pseudo-religious Symbolist art movement. This widely distributed and reproduced poster became more of an emblem of the movement than did any of the paintings that were produced. It depicts three women in evolving states of grace, symbolizing the liberation of the artist from worldly concerns to a higher plane by means of a new art based on beauty and spiritual values. Less significant for its artistic strength than for its ambition as a visual manifesto, the poster remained something of an anomaly but pointed to an important role for this mass medium.

In England, the Arts and Crafts movement had done much to stimulate interest and raise standards in book design, printing, and typography. William Morris founded the Kelmscott Press and was active as a book designer himself (figure 7). But while Morris looked to the Gothic period for inspiration in his attempts to create a unified style in the arts, other designers in the Arts and Crafts movement as well as artists—such as James Abbott McNeill Whistler—turned to the newly discovered art of Japan. In poster design, the Japanese influence was much in evidence in the work of A. A. Turbayne and Aubrey Beardsley. But while Turbayne's poster *Macmillan's Illustrated Standard Novels* (plate 12) displays an obvious Japanese influence, Beardsley's work transforms the influence (and many others) into an intensely personal style (plate 13). Even more than Mucha, Beardsley came to embody the decadent *fin-de-siècle* aspect of Art Nouveau.

Two groups of designers in Great Britain were to exercise a major influence on the medium, particularly on the continent. They were the Beggarstaffs (William Nicholson and James Pryde), who took the pseudonym to differentiate their poster work from their painting, and in Glasgow, the Four (architect Charles Rennie Mackintosh, the Macdonald sisters, and Herbert McNair). Drawing upon the broad flat areas of color and heavy flowing outlines, which Toulouse-Lautrec had adapted from Japanese prints, the Beggarstaffs simplified and abstracted these elements even more in their work. Sometimes, as in their *Hamlet* (plate 17), they would cut out a silhouetted figure and paste it on the poster itself, achieving a powerful and simple monumentality. In contrast to Toulouse-Lautrec, whose perceptive line caught the individual features of his personages in sharp caricature, the Beggarstaffs generalized the individual features of their figures. Their economical and powerful rendering style, combined with clear bold lettering, became perhaps the most important point of departure for the German commercial poster, which emerged some ten years later.

Charles Rennie Mackintosh and his colleagues developed a

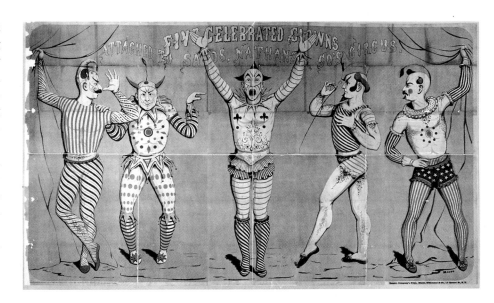

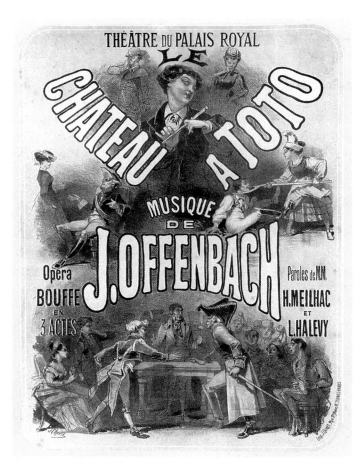

Figure 2. Joseph W. Morse. *Five Celebrated Clowns*. 1856. Woodcut, 82″ × 11′4⅞″. The Library of Congress, Washington, D.C.

Figure 3. Jules Chéret. *Le Chateau a Toto*. 1868. Lithograph, 29½ × 22″. Collection Lucy Broido

Figure 4. Utagawa Kunimasa. *Nakamura Noshio*. 1797. Six-color print, embossed, 14½ × 9¾". Collection Charles H. Chandler

Figure 5. Utagawa Kuniyoshi. *Cats in Various Attitudes*. c. 1843–52. Color woodcut, printed on fan, 8¾ × 11¼". The Raymond A. Bidwell Collection of Prints, Museum of Fine Arts, Springfield, Massachusetts

Figure 6. Édouard Manet. *Champfleury–Les Chats*. 1868. Lithograph, 21⅝ × 17½". Bibliothèque des Arts Décoratifs, Paris

poster style closely related to the decorative detail of his architecture, providing the first important example of the integration of the decorative and graphic arts. It also marks the first entry of the architect-designer—as opposed to the illustrator and painter—into the design of posters, a phenomenon that would significantly transform the medium. While Mackintosh's *The Scottish Musical Review* (plate 14) shares many of the characteristics typical of Art Nouveau—decorative line, flat patterning, and Symbolist motifs—it is also different, evincing a pure quality that came to stand for a new beginning. In contrast to the sense of ennui in the work of the principal European metropolises, the work from Glasgow provided a fresh breeze from the uncorrupted distant provinces. Similarly, the work of Ferdinand Hodler in Switzerland provided a sense of a fresh start. At a time that saw Paul Gauguin travel to Tahiti and others to still-primitive, distant corners of Europe, the idea of a renewal of the arts from the periphery was of considerable interest.

While America had been a pioneer in the illustrated commercial poster, it was not internal evolution but influences from France and Britain that led to the American flowering of the "art" poster in the 1890s. Publishing houses took the lead, advertising their magazines and books. An exhibition of post-

ers organized at the Grolier Club in New York in 1890 made many Americans aware of the work of leading European poster designers. When *Harper's* magazine first commissioned Edward Penfield to do a monthly poster for each new issue (plate 22), competitive instinct prompted others, such as *The Chap Book* (plates 18, 19, 21), to do the same. While formal European influences are apparent—from Morris's Arts and Crafts movement to the works of Toulouse-Lautrec and Bonnard—the American poster exudes a wholesome middle-class propriety quite different from the frivolity, decadence, or sharp caricature of its European counterpart.

Of the American artists, Will Bradley was perhaps the most inventive, but the most fascinating poster in terms of future developments was an unknown designer's *Victor Cycles*, of 1898 (plate 23). In this poster "Ride a Victor" becomes an evenly repeated slogan that hovers like a thin plane on a black ground. A hypnotic figure shrouded in black partly obscures the message. But, as black shroud and black background are ambiguous and undifferentiated, face and slogan begin to float freely. A further, frontal plane, consisting of a complex pattern of thin swirling circles and ellipses, reinforces the hypnotic effect. The American advertising industry's future strategies for disseminating its subliminal messages by endless repetition could not be more clearly—if too blatantly—anticipated here.

In other parts of Europe, Art Nouveau designers produced interesting posters. *Salon des Cent*, by the Belgian painter James Ensor (plate 24), utilizes a jagged line that heightens the emotion of the work, reflecting his own proto-Expressionist style. It throws into relief the Expressionist tendency underlying the work of the Dutch artist Jan Toorop, which, however, also remains linked to the decorative devices of Art Nouveau.

That style's most important contribution to graphics was made by Henry van de Velde, who gave up painting to pursue the applied arts. Inspired to do so by the example of the Arts and Crafts movement he, nevertheless, rejected Morris's Gothic ideal and advocated instead a style expressive of the age. Graphics and typography became the mediating sphere in unifying the fine and applied arts. They also became the most visible method of improving design in the everyday commercial environment. Van de Velde's 1899 designs for advertising, posters, packaging, and letterheads for the Tropon company constituted the first comprehensive design program for a commercial enterprise (figure 8).

But van de Velde's Tropon poster as well as Toorop's *Delftsche Slaolie* (plate 25) also illustrate how Art Nouveau elevated form over content. Its use for commercial products as opposed to cultural events was to be limited by this fact. In contrast, Henri Meunier's early poster for Pollet et Vittet cocoa (plate 35) seems a model of clarity, as does Fritz Boscovits's humorous *Bilz Brause* (plate 34).

The preoccupation of Art Nouveau with mood and symbol is evoked in Jan Preisler's *Worpswede* (plate 33) and Emile Preetorius's *Licht und Schatten* (plate 32). Johannes Sluyters's *Zegepraal* (plate 28) and J. J. Christian Lebeau's *De Magiër* (plate 29), one for a book, the other for a play, reflected the Symbolist legacy of Art Nouveau as well as what seems a peculiarly Dutch tradition: a preoccupation with the frontal figure, arms outstretched, in a transcendental pose. It was a theme that obsessed Mondrian during the same period.

Simplicissimus, a satirical journal that began publication in 1897 in Berlin, became a showcase for some of the most advanced illustrators in Germany. Thomas Theodor Heine's 1897 poster for the magazine (plate 30), featuring a growling bulldog in stark red on a black background, its features exaggerated with a few heavy bold strokes, is a clear anticipation of German Expressionism at its best and stands in contrast to the lighter, more frivolous tone of Josef Rudolf Witzel's poster for the Munich magazine *Jugend* of about the same time (plate 36).

The posters capture the different moods of the two German cultural capitals, a difference that was later to be apparent, although less so, in the work of the two great poster artists Lucian Bernhard and Ludwig Hohlwein.

A poster of a decade later for an automobile company by Akseli Gallen-Kallela, the Finnish artist with strong Berlin connections, is fascinating in its anticipation of future advertising themes (plate 31). Two years before Marinetti's first *Manifesto of Futurism* equated driving and eroticism, Gallen-Kallela did so visually in what may be seen as an updated version (from horses to cars) of the classic abduction motif. From a different point of view he clearly anticipated Madison Avenue's methods for selling cars, perhaps too explicitly (there is some evidence that the poster was never actually used by the company). The title is a play on words: the last word in the name of the company, "Bil aktie Bolaget," has been shortened to "Bol," which means ball—equating car, woman, and plaything.

The integration of text and image, or at least their harmonious coexistence, has always been a fundamental concern for poster artists. In most cases, the text has been hand-lettered, unless, as in Beardsley's *Avenue Theatre, A Comedy of Sighs!* (plate 13), a section was left blank for the addition of information to be printed separately by letterpress. It was an issue

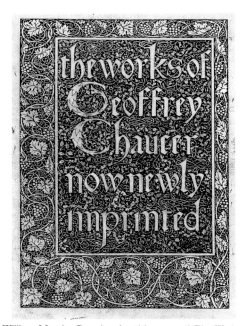

Figure 7. William Morris. Drawing for title page of *The Works of Geoffrey Chaucer*. 1896. Pen and ink on paper, 16½ × 11⅜". The Pierpont Morgan Library, New York

Chéret struggled with and one that Toulouse-Lautrec and Bonnard solved well, as did the Beggarstaffs and the Germans, who chose strong clear type to complement their powerful images. At the height of Art Nouveau, fascinating efforts were made to give the lettering of the text the same decorative and sinuous flow as the design of the poster. Witzel's *Jugend* is an excellent example, with text and image having equal weight. But the most extreme case in point is Hector Guimard's unique poster *Exposition Salon du Figaro, Le Castel Beranger* of 1900 (plate 37). Printed in pastel tones, the decorative, hand-drawn text dominates the whole poster. In the background, in a lighter and different tone, a swirling design in the manner of the architect's decorative ironwork echoes the text. Perhaps the first example of a visually captivating typographic poster, *Le Castel Beranger* foreshadowed the purely typographic poster of the 1920s, albeit in a very different style.

The Vienna Secession, formed in 1897 by a group of artists and architects, was, as the name implies, a faction that broke away from the official artists' organization that dominated exhibition activity. But beyond disagreements about artistic direction, which had caused the formation of a number of *salons des refusés*, the Secession had grander ambitions. Like their contemporaries elsewhere, such as van de Velde, the members of the Secession were concerned with the unity of all the arts, both fine and applied. The formation of the Secession and, subsequently, the Wiener Werkstätte devoted to the applied arts, marked the emergence of Vienna as an important European center of artistic innovation. Posters became a medium that attracted both artists and architects, and Secession and other art exhibitions became their main vehicles. The evolution of the Viennese poster style closely paralleled developments in art, architecture, and the applied arts in Vienna. Gustav Klimt's allegorical Secession poster of 1898 (plate 41) is done in a classical style related to Joseph Maria Olbrich's Secession building design, featured in another poster (plate 42). Koloman Moser's work reflected the influence of Art Nouveau in both its French and Scottish varieties, as well as that of the important Swiss artist Hodler, whose own poster designs are of a later date. The influence of Mackintosh was even more pronounced in interiors and decorative arts: his style was adapted by Josef Hoffmann and Moser, and made more geometric and patternlike. The square became both module and decoration. The love of pattern noticeable in the art of Klimt, in Viennese architecture, and in the decorative arts of the Wiener Werkstätte can be seen in posters of 1902 to 1908, such as those of Ferdinand Andri and Bertold Löffler (plates 44, 45).

The impetus toward geometric order and patterning did not leave typography untouched. Legibility was sacrificed to emphasize the decorative patternlike quality of the text, an urge not dissimilar to the efforts of Art Nouveau but with a very different effect. The early geometric clarity of the furniture and decorative arts of the Wiener Werkstätte became increasingly ornamental and eventually more baroque. The high-minded early ideals of improving the world succumbed to the consumption of goods, as the *haute bourgeoisie* embraced the stylish modern objects of the Werkstätte. The inevitable reaction to relentless polish and decorative excess came in the form of Expressionism, which in its Viennese version was less involved with the primitive and the savage than with the perverse and ugly. The extreme gestures of Oskar Kokoschka, Max Oppenheimer, and Egon Schiele, designed to jolt the *sachertorte* sensibilities of their fellow Viennese (plates 46–48), contrast with the continuing, wholesome, romantic monumental naturalism in Switzerland and the evolution of the tough, straightforward commercial poster in Germany.

This is not to say that Vienna did not have strong advocates of the *sachlich* approach. Ironically, the work of Hohlwein and Bernhard, who contributed the most to the development of the German commercial poster, brings to mind the architect Adolf Loos and his writings on the simple comforts of English dress and on the evolution of artifacts to their natural functional form. However, Hohlwein, who worked in Munich, betrays a certain Viennese influence in posters such as *Deutsches Theater* and *Damenconfectionshaus Mayer Sundheimer* (plates 53, 54), by organizing his text into square blocks that echo the square format of his illustration. In contrast, his work for Hermann Scherrer and Confection Kehl (plates 56–58) presents vignettes of everyday life and text in a direct manner. In another respect, however, he utilized pattern to great effect in these works, imposing broad areas of flat pinstripe or square grid to define the dapper clothes of his models. At the same time, certain elements are rendered three-dimensionally by means of shadows and highlights, creating a tension between flatness and depth. The imposition of pattern to emphasize a flat picture plane closely parallels developments in painting, such as the work of Édouard Vuillard. But the painterly touch of the artist has here been replaced by a crisp, mechanical image.

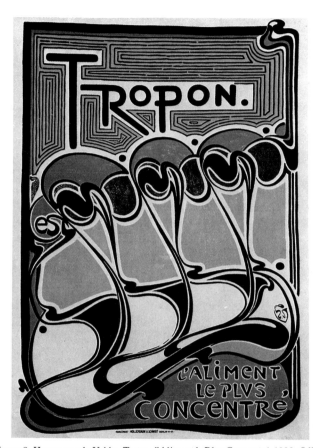

Figure 8. Henry van de Velde. *Tropon l'Aliment le Plus Concentré*. 1899. Offset facsimile of original lithograph, 31⅝ × 21⅜". The Museum of Modern Art, New York. Gift of Tropon-Werke

Figure 9. Peter Behrens. *AEG–Metallfadenlampe*. 1907. Lithograph, 26⅝ × 20¾". Collection Merrill C. Berman

In contrast to Hohlwein, who usually isolated a vignette to represent the product, Bernhard took an even more reductivist and economical approach, showing only the product and the name of the manufacturer. Using brilliant and unexpected colors, and a powerful and simplified composition that juxtaposes image and text, Bernhard created a style that, even more than Hohlwein's, set the tone for subsequent commercial poster design. The Swiss, in particular, were to develop it further, although few equalled the impact of his work. Bernhard was also to inspire his own generation of German designers, among them Ernst Deutsch, Hans Rudi Erdt, Julius E. Gipkens, and Julius Klinger, all of whom contributed to the style. While neither Bernhard nor Hohlwein were directly involved with the Deutscher Werkbund, their work reflects its goals as well as the emergence of Germany as a modern industrial and commercial power.

It is also fascinating to compare their work with that of architect Peter Behrens, one of the Werkbund's founders, who—taking van de Velde's concept for Tropon one step further—provided a comprehensive design program (buildings, products, posters, and other graphics) for the Allgemeine Elektricitaets Gesellschaft, Germany's largest electric company. But Behrens's poster for AEG (figure 9), for all its reduction to pure geometry, is in another respect quite decorative and betrays a strong Viennese influence.

The commercial poster found its modern functional and artistic form in the work of Hohlwein, Bernhard, and their contemporaries. In contrast to the obscure symbolism and formal complexities of Art Nouveau commercial posters or the strong and unusual efforts of the unknown designer of *Victor Cycles* or Gallen-Kallela, Hohlwein and Bernhard provided a reliable straightforward formula. Their own work set an artis-

Figure 10. James Montgomery Flagg. *I Want You for U.S. Army*. 1917. Lithograph, 40¼ × 29½". The Museum of Modern Art, New York. Acquired by exchange

tic standard for the genre at a time when the commercial poster was at its height. It must be remembered that until well into the 1920s the colored lithographic poster was the most powerful vehicle for commercial advertising in existence. There were no radio or television, and journals were essentially confined to black-and-white reproduction.

For similar reasons, the poster became one of the principal and most effective vehicles of government and political propaganda. With the advent of the First World War and subsequent political turmoil, the propaganda poster came into its own. While illustrators produced most of this work—such as James Montgomery Flagg's famous *I Want You for U.S. Army* (figure 10)—the best poster designs were inspired by Bernhard. The boots and gloves that had been used to represent consumer objects became symbols of war, in the form of armor and heavy riding boots. This marked the first modern widespread use in art of parts of the body—the hand, arm, foot, and later the eye and mouth—as symbols. Dada and Surrealism also developed this device, as did Pop art much later.

The ideological conflicts unleashed by the triumph of the Bolsheviks produced handsome examples of extreme paranoia and witty caricature. Rudi Sald's *Die Gefahr des Bolschewismus*

(plate 71), with a knife-wielding skeleton in the foreground and gallows in the background, was in fact a plagiary from the cover of a murder mystery; while the poster by an unknown Russian designer wishing the Bolshevik revolution well on its tenth anniversary (plate 72), is a wonderful satire on the forces of reaction (monarchy, church, imperial army, capitalists, and Uncle Sam) charging the ramparts of communism on the back of a colossal pig.

The postwar years gave new impetus to the spread of modernist aesthetics to the more popular artistic mediums. In Germany, Expressionism in the visual arts, which before the war had flourished in painting and sculpture, after the war spread to architecture (briefly), film, and posters. The range of Expressionist posters shows how the genre was able to draw upon, adapt, and synthesize numerous styles, from the Gothic to Cubism. But unlike the Russian film poster, which drew upon the montage effects of the film medium itself, the German Expressionist film poster was essentially scenographic.

The pictorial influence of Cubism was also to become manifest at a popular level immediately after the war, but to a limited degree. The early posters of E. McKnight Kauffer in England are some of the best examples. Among the most remarkable is Karel Maes's poster of 1922, *De Vertraagde Film* (plate 83), which, in its crisp mechanical form suggesting spinning reels and overlapping transparencies, had close connections to the work of his fellow Belgian artist Victor Servranckx and also to the mechanistic art of Fernand Léger.

In his first *Manifesto of Futurism* Marinetti had written, "We will sing of great crowds excited by work, by pleasure, and by riot . . . of the multicolored polyphonic tides of revolution in the modern capitals . . . of the vibrant nightly fervors of arsenals and shipyards blazing with electric moons."[7] In his poetry he sought to give visual expression to the anarchic energy of war, the big city, and the rioting crowd (figure 11). Setting out to destroy all literary and typographic rules, Marinetti called for the abolition of punctuation, the adverb, and the adjective to break down completely the traditional continuity and order of writing. His poems also offend all traditional criteria for good taste and clarity in layout and design in a way that the lyrical poetry of Stéphane Mallarmé or even Guillaume Apollinaire (figure 12), two other pioneers of free verse, never did. The Futurists also had a particular interest in the medium of print, not just as a vehicle for their poetry but for the purpose of proselytizing their ideas on subjects touching all aspects of life—from sculpture to lust.

Although they produced almost no typographically advanced posters, the revolution the Futurists initiated in typography proved fundamental. Through their influence on Dada and the Russian avant-garde they contributed to the development of the new typography in the 1920s, despite the apparent contrast between their anarchic compositions and the highly structured compositions of the Constructivists.

Futurism's rejection of tradition and its love of anarchy and chance made it an important influence on Dada. This can be seen in the scrambled composition of the text in the poster *Kleine Dada Soirée* of 1922 (plate 84) by Theo van Doesburg and Kurt Schwitters. In another respect there is an important difference. The Futurist typographic poem was usually orchestrated to provide a sense of simultaneity of sounds and events and a feeling of the physical jostling of one element by another. Dada artists, wishing to express chance and the irrational, produced a characteristically random juxtaposition of disparate images, ideograms, and words, emphasizing the discontinuity of the compositional elements (figure 13). The Dadaists' appropriation and use of ideograms—the eye or the hand with pointed finger, among others—would reverberate through subsequent graphics, the latter to the point where it became something of a cliché. Both Futurism and Dada embraced photography and film, two essentially new artistic mediums. Particularly, early Dada experiments with photomontage (figures 14, 15) were instrumental in extending the interest of the avant-garde to the possibilities of the photograph and its combination with typography and text.

Given their diversity, there was a remarkable amount of animated contact and fruitful intercourse among the various avant-garde groups after the war. This was, no doubt, reinforced by their exhilaration in finding like minds addressing common problems from different directions, especially after the isolation caused by four years of hostilities. The need to communicate and proselytize was great. Small avant-garde journals became the favored vehicles for projecting and exchanging ideas: *Dada* in Zurich; *De Stijl* and *Mecano* in the Netherlands; *LEF* and *Novyi LEF* in Russia; *Ma* in Hungary; *G, Merz, Veshch/Gegenstand/Objet*, and *Der Dada* in Germany; *Blok* in Poland; and *L'Esprit Nouveau* in France (figure 16). Most of them also provided showcases for typographic experimentation, and their group exhibitions and events spawned handbills and posters.

LA CRAVATE ET LA MONTRE

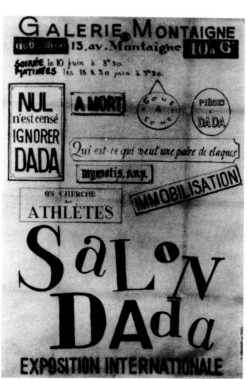

Figure 11. Filippo Tommaso Marinetti. Page from *Les Mots en Liberté Futuristes*. Milan: Edizione Futuriste di "Poesia," 1919. Letterpress, 13⅜ × 9¼". The Museum of Modern Art, New York. Gift of Philip Johnson

Figure 12. Guillaume Apollinaire. Page from *Calligrammes* (1917). Paris: Librairie Gallimard, 1930. Letterpress, 13⅛ × 9⅞". The Museum of Modern Art, New York. The Louis E. Stern Collection

Figure 13. Tristan Tzara. *Salon Dada*. 1921. Offset lithograph, 46 × 30⅛". Collection Elaine Lustig Cohen

Figure 14. George Grosz and John Heartfield. *Leben und Treiben in Universal-
City*. 1919. Photomontage. Whereabouts
unknown

Figure 15. Raoul Hausmann. *La Critique
d'Art*. 1919. Photomontage, 12⅜ × 9¾".
Collection Fordemberge

A strange confluence of movements (Dada, de Stijl, and Constructivism) and individuals (van Doesburg, Schwitters, and El Lissitzky among them) came, in fact, to form a loose coalition of disparate interests. They did share an antipathy toward Expressionism, which emphasized individual emotion. But otherwise Dada and de Stijl or, for that matter, Dada and Constructivism seemed to have little in common. However, the period witnessed van Doesburg, de Stijl's chief propagandist, writing Dada poetry under the pseudonym L. K. Bonset, as well as close collaborations between El Lissitzky and the Dadaist Schwitters in *Merz*. Representation in one another's journals was a common feature of the period, as were such events as the Congress of the Constructivists (which included the Dadaists Jean Arp and Tristan Tzara, among others), organized by van Doesburg in 1922 in Weimar, the location of the Bauhaus, which was still under strong Expressionist influence.

In this intense interaction between the various avant-garde movements after the war, the Russian artist El Lissitzky became the greatest single influence on the new typography. Early Dadaist typographic experiments were too diverse, crystallizing a sensibility but not a style; and early de Stijl graphics, employing heavy woodblock letters, continued to express handicrafts and, like the earlier Viennese work, sacrificed legibility for formal and decorative effect. El Lissitzky, who had trained as an architect in Darmstadt, had become interested in book design while teaching at the Vitebsk art school, and produced some Jewish picture books in a style similar to that of Marc Chagall, then head of the school. In 1919 he met Kasimir Malevich who also taught at Vitebsk. Adapting Malevich's Suprematist style of dynamic, floating abstract planes to typography, El Lissitzky produced one of the first completely abstract posters, *Beat the Whites with the Red Wedge* (figure 17). This was followed in 1920 by his famous children's story *The Tale of 2 Squares*. Moving to Berlin in 1921, El Lissitzky (with the poet Ilya Ehrenburg) started the trilingual magazine *Veshch/Gegenstand/Objet*, which, among other things, served as a vehicle for his typographic designs. Equally important was his design for the poet Vladimir Mayakovsky's *For Reading Out Loud* of 1923 (figure 18). El Lissitzky's work exercised an immediate and important influence on van Doesburg, Schwitters, and perhaps most important, László Moholy-Nagy.

El Lissitzky's graphic design work progressed from his early efforts (directly indebted to Suprematist painting) to more purely typographic design. A prolific synthesizer, he was also influenced by Dadaist works such as the first cover for *Der Dada* of 1919 by Raoul Hausmann, and by examples of de Stijl. His principal contribution to the new typography was its dynamic and mechanical geometric order, derived from the Suprematist language of planes in space. The new typographic compositions were asymmetrical, often with a strong emphasis on the diagonal, with letters, forms, words, and heavy ruled lines floating on a uniformly colored background. Different typefaces and type sizes were juxtaposed (an influence from Dada). Elements often overlapped and/or interlocked. The combination of black, red, and white gave the works striking visual as well as revolutionary effect. Summing up the mechanical impersonal aspirations of the new objectivity, El Lissitzky wrote, "For modern advertisement and for the modern exponent of form the individual element—the artist's 'own touch'—is of absolutely no consequence."[8]

Along with the avant-garde interest in new typography went an interest in the new mediums of film and photography. The postwar years saw the emergence of film as a form of mass entertainment and the extension of photography in the form of the illustrated photojournal. Although the halftone process of photographic reproduction had been invented in 1880, its widespread use as a replacement for engraved illustrations had to await further technical improvement and the end of the First World War. Because of technical deficiencies in the printing process, photographic reproductions were for a long time regarded as inferior to engravings. For similar reasons, the photographic poster remained a rarity until the 1920s.

To the members of the avant-garde, photography and film had a double appeal in their objectivity and mass reproducibility. They also had a popular appeal that abstract design in itself did not enjoy. Of the new mediums, El Lissitzky said, "The invention of easel-pictures produced great works of art, but their effectiveness has been lost. The cinema and the illustrated weekly magazine have triumphed."[9]

The mass of photographic material generated by the illustrated press became the raw material of a new art form: photomontage. The German Dadaists Raoul Hausmann, John Heartfield, and Hannah Höch exploited its possibilities, as did the Russians Alexander Rodchenko, Gustav Klutsis, and others. Who did it first is a moot point, as its roots go back to the nineteenth century. The new technique allowed displacement and juxtapositions, assemblages and collages of infinite variety. It was used for humorous, political, or surreal purposes. Photomontage created a new kind of poster, from Heartfield's political posters to Moholy-Nagy's brilliant integration of photography, typography, and drawing in his *Pneumatik* (figure 19), a poster proposal of 1923.

Photography provided another useful technique, the photogram, involving the direct exposure of photographic paper, first exploited by the Dada artist Christian Schad in his Schadograms and by the American Man Ray. Its relevance to the art of the poster was first made clear by El Lissitzky in his 1924 poster proposal, *Pelikan Tinte* (figure 20).

When Johannes Itten (figure 21), who taught the Bauhaus Preliminary Course with an emphasis on individual expression, was succeeded by Moholy-Nagy in 1923, the Bauhaus moved decisively toward the rational Constructivist style for which it became known. The new direction proved more fruitful in terms of the school's broad ambitious goals, and helped bring them into clearer focus. Moholy-Nagy focused on typography,

Figure 16. Avant-garde magazines, left to right, first row: *Ma* (Hungary), 1922; *Merz* (Germany), 1923, cover by Kurt Schwitters; *Der Dada* (Germany), 1919, cover by Raoul Hausmann; second row: *G* (Germany), 1926; *Novyi LEF* (Russia), 1928, cover by Alexander Rodchenko; *Blok* (Poland), 1924, cover by Teresa Zarnowerowna; *Veshch/Gegenstand/Objet* (Germany), 1922, cover by El Lissitzky; third row: *De Stijl* (the Netherlands), 1917, cover by Vilmos Huszar; *Mecano* (the Netherlands), 1923, cover by Theo van Doesburg; *L'Esprit Nouveau* (France), 1922

photography, photomontage, and the photogram. While no official courses in typography or photography existed at the Bauhaus until its move to Dessau in 1925, Moholy-Nagy took charge of the existing printing shop (used for Bauhaus publicity) and encouraged his students—among them Josef Albers, Herbert Bayer, and Joost Schmidt—to use it. Oskar Schlemmer produced a series of posters in his own distinctive mechano-figural style. In Dessau, a number of former students were appointed masters, and typography became part of the curriculum. Schmidt taught a compulsory course in lettering, and Bayer became head of the print workshop.

Bayer's two posters of 1926, for a Hans Poelzig lecture and a Wassily Kandinsky exhibition (plates 93, 95), represent the high classicism of the Bauhaus period, building on a typographic style partly evolved by Moholy-Nagy in the Bauhaus publications (figure 22). In comparison, Schmidt's Bauhaus poster of 1923 (plate 91), with its abstracted anthropomorphism, still seems tentative and El Lissitzky's Constructivist work too experimental. By 1927–28 the typographic poster was moving in new directions involving color, as in a modular Leipzig exhibition poster by Bayer of 1927 and F. H. Wenzel's *Schau Fenster Schau* (plates 96, 97). Walter Dexel, an artist and graphic designer strongly influenced by the Bauhaus but working outside of it, aspired to a straightforward clarity similar to that of Bayer in his poster *Verwende Stets nur Gas* of 1924 (plate 94). But he became more playful in *Fotografie der Gegenwart* of 1929, with its mirror-image type (plate 98), a theme that fascinated many of the designers of the period.

Typography at the Bauhaus was not confined to book and poster design, although the fourteen Bauhaus books published between 1925 and 1930 represented a major typographic contribution, as well as a theoretical one, to the whole field of design. Bayer and Albers designed new sans serif typefaces based on geometric shapes and only in lowercase letters, a mannerism of the period which saw it as both more egalitarian and utilitarian (Gropius wrote all his letters without capitals, as did Bertolt Brecht). Bayer's Universal type and Albers's stencils were developed with display and poster design very much in mind (figures 23, 24). In printing and book design the Bauhaus overwhelmingly favored sans serif lettering. While it is arguable whether sans serif text is more legible, it has a clean, functional look. All the Bauhaus publications, as well as most progressive modern printing of this period, are in sans serif type.

In accordance with the ideals of the Deutscher Werkbund,

Figure 17. El Lissitzky. Facsimile of *Beat the Whites with the Red Wedge*. 1919. Offset lithograph, 19½ × 28″. The Museum of Modern Art Library, New York

the Bauhaus sought to work closely with industry. Indicative of this relationship was the course in advertising art held at the Bauhaus in 1927 by the Association of German Advertising Specialists. The Bauhaus was not alone in bridging the gap from avant-garde art to commercial advertising. Schwitters set up his own advertising company, and in 1927 he formed the Ring der Neuer Werbegestalter (Circle of New Advertising

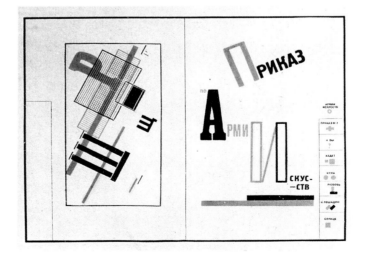

Figure 18. El Lissitzky. Two pages from *For Reading Out Loud* by Vladimir Mayakovsky. Berlin: R.S.F.S.R. State Publishing, 1923. Letterpress, 10¼ × 7″. The Museum of Modern Art, New York. Gift of Philip Johnson

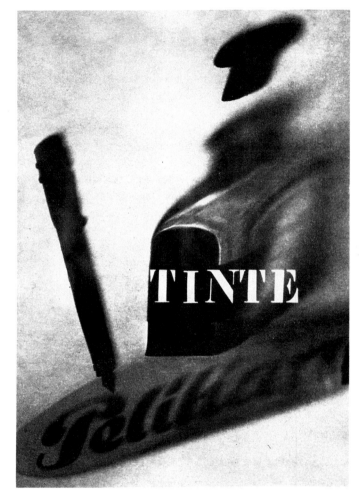

Figure 19. László Moholy-Nagy. *Pneumatik*. 1923. Photomontage with graphic elements. Whereabouts unknown

Figure 20. El Lissitzky. *Pelikan Tinte*. 1924. Photogram, 8⅜ × 5⅞″. Collection Thea Berggren

Designers) with Willi Baumeister, Jan Tschichold, and Friedrich Vordemberge-Gildewart, among others.

The rapid transition taking place in poster and graphic design in this period was reflected by the demise in 1921 of the highly influential journal *Das Plakat*, which had been oriented toward collectors and had in its day championed Bernhard and Hohlwein. Its owner, Hans Sachs, a dentist and poster enthusiast, had amassed what was then the largest poster collection in the world. Four years later, in 1925, *Gebrauchsgraphik*, a journal of international advertising art, began publication with extensive articles on both the new typography and on the new arts of advertising and product photography. Modern graphic

design had come of age, and the innovations of the avant-garde were rapidly being appropriated and adapted to commerce.

Tschichold, one of the few designers who came to the new typography from a typographical background, was instrumental in this process. After he saw the Weimar Bauhaus exhibition *Art and Technics, A New Unity* in 1923, Tschichold became a convert. In 1925, at age twenty-three, he published the article "Elementare Typographie" in the printing trade journal *Typographische Mitteilungen*, which introduced the new Constructivist-inspired typography to a wide audience of professional printers. In 1928 he published *Die Neue Typographie*, and in 1935, *Typographische Gestaltung (Asymmetrical Typography)*, both influential books that sought to explain and codify the new typography. Tschichold's importance was not only as a proselytizer for the new typography but, equally, as a practitioner who refined it. His film posters for the Phoebus Palast theater of 1927, incorporating asymmetrical balance, diagonal layout, photomontage, and text, were highly influential. They parallel work done at the Bauhaus by Max Burchartz. However, both Tschichold's *Die Frau ohne Namen* (plate 100) and Burchartz's *Tanz Festspiele* (plate 101) have their genesis in the photomontages of Moholy-Nagy.

Other photographic posters were documentary in nature, such as Helmut Kurtz's *Ausstellung Neue Haus-Wirtschaft* of 1930, which made a montage of new commercial photographs of modern household artifacts (plate 104). Powerful commentary could be achieved by such basic methods as overprinting a red **X** over a photograph of a traditional interior, as in the poster by an unknown designer for the Deutscher Werkbund exhibition of 1927 in Stuttgart (plate 103). The possible range of invention and fertile combinations was formidable. Johannes Molzahn's coordinated series of posters for the Breslau Werkbund exhibition of 1929 juxtaposes the elegant large logo with, in one poster, a montage of trade skills, and in another, a map of the fairgrounds (plates 105, 106). Bayer drew a surreal abstract landscape, into which he inserted the small figure of a man in his *Section Allemande* poster of 1930 (plate 109). In *IBA* (plate 107) he appropriated typewriter type, a strategy similar to that of Paul Schuitema's for *ANVV* (plate 108), which consists of what appears to be a section of an addressed envelope cover, complete with stamps and labels.

In the Netherlands, the artist Bart van der Leck made an important contribution with several abstract posters in 1919 (figure 25). Like his paintings and the work of a number of other de Stijl artists at this time, they retain a reference to the object represented. It is fascinating to see the beginning of the process of abstraction (seemingly under Egyptian influence) in his poster for the Batavier-Line of c. 1915 (plate 110). Christa Ehrlich, Vilmos Huszar, and Hendrikus Wijdeveld, as well as Gerard Baksteen, defined the 1920s graphic look in the Netherlands, which for all its abstraction retained a refined, handcrafted, and decorative appearance.

Piet Zwart, an architect and furniture designer, became the most inventive exponent of the new Constructivist typography in the Netherlands. Unfortunately, he made very few posters, the best known being *ITF* for a film exhibition of 1928 (plate 114), which elegantly combines the asymmetrical geometry of

de Stijl with a drawing of a film strip viewed by a pair of eyes. However, most of Zwart's inventive work was done for brochures and magazine advertisements for commercial clients, particularly NKF (figure 26), a cable manufacturer. His career illuminates the gradual move of the leading designers into other aspects of graphic design. The main vehicle for commercial advertising became the magazines and journals. The poster, dominant into the early 1920s, was to lose its central role, owing to technical advances in magazine printing.

The 1920s saw the emergence of modern Swiss graphic design, which has continued as a major force in the field to the present day. The early work of Burkhard, Ernst Keller, Niklaus Stoecklin, and Wilhelm Wenk in typographic posters—some using an elegant calligraphic type—contributed to the growth of the genre's formal possibilities. The monumental and highly ordered typographic posters of Theo H. Ballmer of 1928, which today still seem to embody enlightened modern corporate graphics (plates 119–122), reflect his Bauhaus training. Other works by Jean Arp, Otto Baumberger, Alexey Brodovitch, and Walter Cyliax (not all of them Swiss) indicate the spread and appropriation of the new, elegant geometric abstraction. Tschichold's move from Germany to Switzerland

Figure 21. Johannes Itten. *Gruss Heil Herzen*. 1924. Lithograph, 14 × 9⅞″. The Museum of Modern Art, New York. Gift of Samuel A. Berger

Figure 22. László Moholy-Nagy. Title spread from *Malerei, Photographie, Film*. Munich: Albert Langen Verlag, 1925. The Museum of Modern Art, New York

Figure 23. Herbert Bayer. Universal Type. 1925

Figure 24. Josef Albers. Bauhaus Lettering Set. 1926–31. Opaque white glass mounted on yellow wood, 24 × 24″. The Museum of Modern Art, New York. Gift of the designer

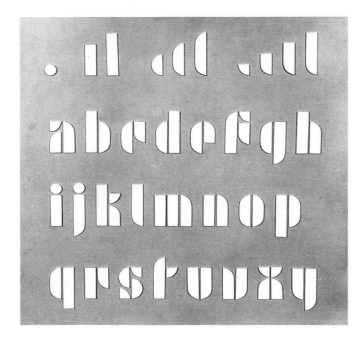

in 1933 capped the cross-fertilization of German and Swiss design. His minimalist Swiss work, such as the *Konstruktivisten* poster of 1937 (plate 127), represents perhaps the ultimate refinement of the new style and has close connections to the work of the Swiss designer Max Bill, who, like Ballmer, studied at the Bauhaus.

El Lissitzky's enthusiasm for typography and book and poster design, photography, and film was not an isolated Russian phenomenon. It was shared by many members of the Russian avant-garde. The revolutionary regime's need to arouse, educate, and transform the consciousness of the masses provided a great demand for these mediums. Although apparently Lenin took a dim view of avant-garde abstraction, he gave Anatole Lunacharsky, the new minister of culture and a modernist sympathizer, a free hand to recruit the avant-garde to the cause of the revolution. Posters, billboards, handbills, anything that could communicate visually, became of primary significance for a vast country with many languages and a high rate of illiteracy.

Vladimir Mayakovsky, the avant-garde poet and artist, coordinated the first, and one of the most significant, efforts of the new regime, the ROSTA[10] window-poster campaign. Mayakovsky developed a satirical poster style of stock characters that built on the traditional *lubok*, a crude peasant style of woodblock printing featuring religious and folk themes (figure 27). While the Bolsheviks had come to power in 1917, efforts by various White Army factions to regain power created an unstable situation until the early 1920s. Empty store windows were used to inform and exhort the populace to maintain its revolutionary fervor.

The ROSTA campaign also produced important efforts such as *What Have You Done for the Front?* (figure 28), probably by Malevich. Essentially a Suprematist composition with text added, it presumably served as inspiration for El Lissitzky, but also highlights El Lissitzky's own important contribution in making typography an integral design element of his *Beat the Whites with the Red Wedge* (see figure 17).

Alexander Rodchenko, who taught at the VKhUTEMAS[11] in Moscow, was central to the development of avant-garde graphics in Russia. Strongly influenced by Malevich and Tatlin (as were so many other Russian artists), in 1921 he and twenty-five other Constructivist artists, later called Productivists, announced that they would abandon pure art in favor of the applied arts. While also designing furniture and clothing, Rodchenko made a major contribution in typography and photography. His many graphic activities included designing animated film titles for Dziga Vertov's newsreels, covers and graphics for the avant-garde journals *LEF* and *Novyi LEF* (see figure 16), a series of photomontages to illustrate Mayakovsky's poem *Pro Eto* (figure 29), book covers, a collaboration with Mayakovsky (who supplied the text) for a series of commercial posters (dubbed by the latter "poetry of the streets"), and film posters. Beginning in 1924 he also became increasingly involved in photography, an interest he shared with Moholy-Nagy and Bayer (he began to correspond with the former in 1923). Rodchenko became the chief Russian exponent of a new photography that emphasized unconventional views (figure 30) as well as the play of shadow and light. The angled shot from below, which tended to monumentalize figures, became conventionalized by the communist regime with which it found favor after other avant-garde practices had been suppressed. The propaganda posters of Klutsis of the early 1930s and photographic work by Rodchenko and El Lissitzky

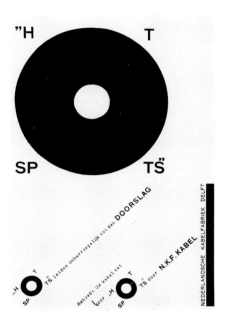

Figure 25. Bart van der Leck. *Tentoonstelling v.d. Leck.* 1919. Lithograph, 45⅝ × 22". Collection Josef Müller-Brockmann, Switzerland

Figure 26. Piet Zwart. *"Hot Spots"* (Advertisement for NKF cable works). 1926. Letterpress, 10 × 6½". The Museum of Modern Art, New York. Gift of Philip Johnson

documenting industrialization, which appeared in the magazine *USSR in Construction*, represented the power of this genre at its best.

Under Soviet auspices the film industry was encouraged as a leading communications medium, and under Lenin's new economic policy many foreign films were imported. Documentary, educational, propaganda, and entertainment films were produced. The work of masters of the medium such as Sergei Eisenstein and Vertov was encouraged. The establishment of a separate department for the production of posters within Sov Kino, which ran the nationalized Russian film industry, was to be of fundamental importance to the development of the Russian film poster between 1924 and 1930. The head of poster production, an artist named Yakov Ruklevsky, recruited a brilliant group of avant-garde Constructivist designers. Of these the most prolific and talented were the brothers Vladimir and Georgii Stenberg, who had already made a name for themselves as sculptors. Others included Anatoli Belski, Josif Bograd, Grigory Borisov, Mikhail Dlugash, Josif Gerasimovich, Anton Lavinsky, Alexandr Naumov, Nikolai Prusakov, Grigory Rychkov, and Leonid Voronov.

The film medium itself influenced the poster genre. The splice, the closeup, simultaneity, juxtaposition, and double exposure all became techniques utilized by poster artists. Rodchenko's compositional technique and photomontage were

Figure 27. Vladimir Mayakovsky. Poster for ROSTA (Russian Telegraph Agency). December 1920

Figure 28. Kasimir Malevich (?). *What Have You Done for the Front?* Poster for ROSTA (Russian Telegraph Agency). 1919

also an important influence. In his commercial posters of 1923 he had evolved a powerful axial format that gave an essentially symmetrical structure to his work, such as one of his advertisements for the Gum department store (figure 31). With the basic order in place, asymmetries could be introduced, such as

a montage of figures, as in one of his detective-story covers (figure 32). The slash lines used here became another favored device (often used as the diagonal) to present different scenes in the same poster.

While techniques of film and photomontage were the point of departure for their posters, the Stenberg brothers, masters of color and the lithographic process, preferred to draw their images. The facilities available for printing photographic images simply did not give them the sharpness and color they desired. However, the photographic quality of their renderings was achieved by a primitive method of projecting film and photographic images to the desired size and then drawing over them.

On their poster for Walter Ruttmann's documentary film *Symphony of a Great City* (plate 137) the Stenbergs adapted a photomontage by the photographer Umbo, featuring a journalist with his camera, typewriter, pen, and watch, and then added text and a modern skyscraper. In the poster for the film *Forced Labor* (plate 140), they drew a filmstrip with one frame enlarged by a magnifying glass; and in the posters *The Three-Million Case* and *Pounded Cutlet* (plates 141, 142) the rendering appears to mimic the flickering effect of film running out of synchronization, in order to achieve a sense of tension and movement. Similarly, El Lissitzky in *USSR Russische Ausstellung* (plate 149) drew his images, although they suggest the photographic technique of double exposure.

When photomontage was actually reproduced in photographic form, as in the inventive poster *I Hurry to See Khaz Push* (plate 144) by Borisov and Prusakov, or *Pipe of the Communards* (plate 145) by Anatoli Belski, it was often used as texture to define a particular shape or object (the bicyclist and the smoke) as well as to add a further narrative dimension. On the other hand, Klutsis preferred large, grainy, crudely reproduced photographic images and combined them with strong red backgrounds to achieve a revolutionary effect (plates 150–152).

What is most remarkable about the Russian film posters of the 1920s is the successful fusion of avant-garde practice and popular culture. By drawing on film and photography, the posters retained the figurative dimension. But the inventive compositional techniques, juxtapositions of images, and uses of color and texture transcended popular taste. The other striking aspect of these posters is the sense of humor and playfulness they project at a time when the avant-garde was serious and ideological.

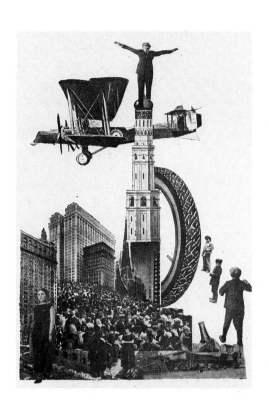

Figure 29. Alexander Rodchenko. Photomontage from *Pro Eto* (*About This*), a poem by Vladimir Mayakovsky. Moscow: State Publications, 1923. Letterpress, 9 × 6″. The Museum of Modern Art, New York. Gift of Philip Johnson

Figure 30. Alexander Rodchenko. *Girl with Leica*. 1934. Photograph, 15¾ × 11⅜″. Collection Gmurzynska, Cologne

Figure 31. Alexander Rodchenko. Advertisement for Gum department store. 1923

Figure 32. Alexander Rodchenko. Design for the cover of *The Mask of Revenge*, a detective story. Moscow: State Publications, 1924

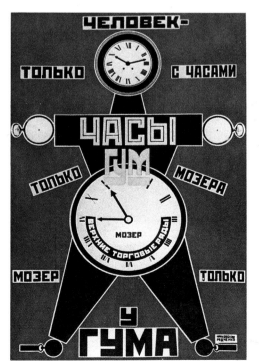

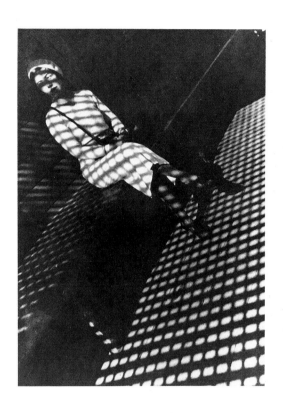

If the political posters of Gustav Klutsis sought to reflect the euphoria of collective experience in building up a new social order and industrializing a backward country, the posters of A. M. Cassandre in bourgeois France and, in general, those of the 1930s in the West (among the victorious Allies) sought to reflect the euphoria of the new hectic pace of life and the new freedom in countries increasingly industrialized, middle-class, and consumer-oriented. Cassandre's *La Route Bleue, Étoile du Nord* (plates 153, 154), and many other railway posters, as well as the posters of his contemporaries Paul Colin, Pierre Fix-Masseau, J. P. Junot, and Charles Loupot, beautifully symbolize the lure of fast travel. Unlike today, belching smokestacks were then a symbol of progress, as of course were whirling gears, captured in all their muscular power by E. McKnight Kauffer in his maquette for *Metropolis* or in his work for the London Regional Transport Authority (plates 165–167).

While Germany suffered the trauma of defeat and financial crisis, and Russia was preoccupied with building a new revolutionary society, France and Britain set about picking up the pieces and getting on with enjoying life. There was generally a positive attitude toward industrialization and the forms it generated, and no desire to radically change the world, only a wish to facilitate the coming of the new age.

School of Paris modernism provided an important formal and ideological basis for the work of poster artists, particularly Cassandre and Kauffer. Léger and the Purists—Ozenfant and Le Corbusier—were the most important points of departure. While neither Le Corbusier nor Ozenfant was actively involved in graphic design (in fact, *L'Esprit Nouveau* had a rather conservative appearance), they had a very real interest in the print mediums, whose revolutionary impact they recognized. Just as they sought to make their readers aware of the power of the new, vernacular industrial architecture they sought to make them aware of the beauty of machines and industrially produced objects through "found" advertising photographs and prospectuses, which they recycled as cryptic visual comments in their magazine. A series of articles in *L'Esprit Nouveau* titled "Eyes Which Do Not See," in 1921–22, focused on ocean liners, airplanes, and cars as presenting the new forms of modern life rationally arrived at. While the authors wanted to focus on the process by which these had been designed, their illustrations provided an immediate and powerful iconography for the new aesthetic (figure 33).

The interest in engineering forms was not new (the Futurists had extolled them), but the formal means of presenting them were. The Futurists had adapted Cubism to show movement and simultaneity, also seeking to capture the chaos and tumult of the new, urban industrial landscape. The postwar French artists fused Cubism with the French classical tradition to create monumental still-life and landscape art of modern industrial forms that extolled both volumetric articulation and layering. While the Purists, on the one hand, confined themselves almost solely to still-life painting of *objets trouvés*—innocuous everyday mass-produced objects such as bottles, glasses, and plates—others, among them the American Precisionists, depicted industrial landscapes, closely cropped views of ocean liners, factory smokestacks, or ventilators.

Léger was not interested in the obvious monumental forms of industrialism but, rather, in smaller, everyday objects or details such as gears. Nor was his interest exclusively industrial: he rendered with equal care a classical baluster. Léger's fusion of Cubism with volumetric articulation, and his style of impersonal rendering, shading, and clarity of outline was particularly suited to lithography and mechanical reproduction, and artists such as Cassandre and Kauffer made the most of it, each adapting it to suit his own needs. Léger himself designed only two posters, one for the film *La Roue* (figure 34), by Abel Gance, the other for the film *L'Inhumanité*, by Marcel Herbier (neither one realized). For all the brilliance with which they integrated typography with mechanical imagery, these maquettes are essentially extensions of Léger's paintings.

What makes the work of Cassandre and Kauffer extraordinary is the way in which it reduces the complexity of the work of Léger or the Purists, among others, to essentials—to instantly graspable iconic forms. Their poster work, of course, had a very immediate, functional purpose: to catch the attention of the populace and to sell a product. For this they utilized the new visual language and its formal compositional means to brilliant effect.

The London Regional Transport Authority was an enlightened client for graphic design, and commissioned a whole series of posters from Kauffer and from unlikely artists such as Man Ray, whose poster with an Underground symbol floating like a planet in the cosmos (plate 168) represents an eerie symbolism and an ironic one, given the earthbound nature of the London subway system. The typeface used by Man Ray was one of the first modern sans serif faces, which had been commissioned in 1915 for the Underground from the calligrapher Edward Johnson.

Figure 33. Turbines, from *L'Esprit Nouveau*. No. 24, 1925. The Museum of Modern Art Library, New York

Figure 34. Fernand Léger. Maquette for a poster for *La Roue*. 1920. Gouache, 12¼ × 9⅝". Private collection

With the exception of isolated examples or where elements of photomontage are used, the photographic poster did not become widespread until the mid-1930s. Herbert Matter's Swiss travel posters (plates 179, 180) were pioneers in this regard, as was Xanti Schawinsky's 1934 poster for Olivetti (plate 187). Matter's works are actually photomontages that appear to be fortuitously composed photographs. While, at first glance these posters seem to be color photographs, they are in fact tinted black-and-white images. Other examples are the *BMW Motorräder* poster by Popp-Kircheim of c. 1935 (plate 176) and the fascinating poster for Goodyear tires of c. 1932 (plate 177), where a colossal tire is inserted among a row of parked cars, and the volumetric typography is neatly laid out in perspective and integrated into the street scene.

From approximately 1920 onward the Swiss developed a style of commercial poster that built upon the work of Lucian Bernhard, featuring only the product and brand name. However, unlike Bernhard, their rendering style tended to imitate photography, as in the work of Baumberger, Alex W. Diggelmann, and Pierre Gauchat. While extremely handsome, this did make the Swiss product posters more prosaic and middle-class than the powerfully rendered work of Bernhard. In one respect Baumberger took Bernhard's formula a step further in *PKZ*, a poster of 1923 (plate 188). A closeup view of a man's tweed jacket, it features only the store label on the lapel of the coat. Other formal variations on this genre continued into the late 1940s.

The rise of fascism in Europe, among other things, was to cause a significant transfer of artistic talent to America in the 1930s and early 1940s. Mondrian and Marcel Duchamp settled in New York. The architects Gropius and Marcel Breuer came to teach at Harvard, and Ludwig Mies van der Rohe to Armour Institute (later Illinois Institute of Technology). Among the many immigrants in graphics and design were Bayer, Bernhard, Joseph Binder, Brodovitch, Jean Carlu, Gyorgy Kepes, Leo Lionni, Matter, Moholy-Nagy, Schawinsky, and Latislav Sutnar. Through their influence as teachers they contributed to America's widespread acceptance of modernism in the postwar years.

As is evident from the work of Carlu and Lionni, a number of these designers found immediate use for their talents designing war posters. The Museum of Modern Art was one of the sponsors of a war-poster competition in 1942 won by Victor Ancona and Karl Koehler with *This Is the Enemy*, featuring a caricature of a Nazi with a hanged man reflected in his eyeglasses (plate 193). Ironically, a German poster designed by Hohlwein as early as 1929 for the fascistic veterans' Stahlhelm Party and later used as a campaign poster by the Nazis in 1932, presents an even more frightening picture (plate 192). Among the most memorable American war posters is Ben Shahn's *This Is Nazi Brutality* of 1943 (plate 194), with its grim teletype message.

The end of the war brought other serious issues to the fore, among them voter registration and civil rights (plate 198), polio, and nuclear annihilation. While Bayer's *Polio Research* and *Das Wunder des Lebens* (plates 199, 200) were eloquent reminders of the rapid and impressive scientific and medical advances taking place in this period, Hans Erni's early protest against atomic war (plate 201) makes clear that these advances were double-edged.

The reaction against avant-garde modernism in the 1930s, as well as the enormous destruction and dislocations caused by the Second World War, led to a disruption of the modernist enterprise. However, the more "traditional" artistic tastes of the fascist and communist regimes gave the modern movement a whole new status after the war: it emerged as the preferred art of the free democratic world.

Painters of the School of Paris gained new international recognition. The loosening of the strict, formal compositional concerns of the 1930s became even more pronounced after the war, when art moved toward a lyrical abstraction with a new emphasis on painterly qualities such as texture and the free gesture of the artist's hand. This new sensibility, in Paris and elsewhere, was to exercise considerable influence on graphic designers. In this regard one thinks especially of the cutouts of Henri Matisse, the playful biomorphism of Joan Miró, and the earlier, lyrical drawings and watercolors of Paul Klee. In general, the brightly colored, the playful, and the informal came to dominate postwar European art and graphic design. Instead of the call for a new order of the previous generation, the emphasis was on light entertainment, now presented in the context of modernism. Indicative of one aspect of the new spirit was the work of Raymond Savignac (figure 35), whose simplified illustration style spread from France as far as Poland and the United States. Another aspect, more clearly related to developments in painting, was represented by the work of the American Paul Rand (figure 36).

At the same time, Bauhaus and Constructivist influences retained a foothold in the United States (owing to the influence of the expatriate designers) and in Switzerland, where Bill and Ballmer, among others, were still active as practitioners and pedagogues. Switzerland, which consolidated and developed further this formalist inheritance, emerged in the late 1950s and 1960s as perhaps the most influential center of graphic design. Many factors contributed to making Swiss graphics internationally preeminent. Among these were a technically advanced and highly skilled printing industry that had continued to develop while the rest of Europe was devastated by the war, and a strong tradition of graphic design going back to the beginning of the century that had been further nurtured by extensive contact with the Bauhaus. The active encouragement of poster design by the Swiss government, at national and local levels, and the institution of an annual competition to promote poster design, were significant, as were the foundings of such important journals as *Graphis* in 1944 and *New Graphic Design* in 1958. The schools of applied arts in Basel and in Zurich became internationally important educational centers for graphic design. A number of new typefaces were developed in the 1950s by Swiss designers. The most popular was known as Helvetica, a refined version of Akzidenz Grotesk, a nineteenth-century sans serif typeface. Its widespread use became integral to the clarity and easy legibility of the Swiss graphic style.

Among the younger Swiss designers who emerged in the 1950s as important innovators were Armin Hofmann and Josef Müller-Brockmann, who taught at Basel and Zurich, respectively. Müller-Brockmann's *Musica Viva* and Hofmann's exhibition poster *Robert Jacobsen, Serge Poliakoff* (plates 227, 228) demonstrate continuity with the traditions of the 1920s as well as the rigor with which they pursued their craft. They also made a major contribution in combining typography and photography to achieve a powerful visual impact. Hofmann's *Wilhelm Tell* (plate 229), Müller-Brockmann's plea for less noise pollution, *Weniger Lärm* (plate 232), and Karl Gerstner's political poster *Auch Du bist liberal* (plate 233) are examples of the genre. Two purely typographic posters are Müller-Brockmann's *Der Film* (plate 230), which achieves a sense of movement through overlapping type, and the somewhat later poster by Max Huber for the Gran Premio automobile race at Monza, with its blurred type suggesting speeding cars (plate 231).

Just as American corporations adopted modern architecture in the 1950s, they adopted modern graphic design, which gradually went beyond the sponsorship of poster campaigns to the development of a uniform graphic identity for a whole corporation. The pioneering efforts of Tropon and AEG at the beginning of the century were finally becoming a reality in the commercial field. Crisp, gridded, neatly organized graphics— simple and abstract—suited the corporate world just as glass-and-steel curtain-wall architecture did. It was coolly anonymous and exuded efficiency and economy. In the process, of course, avant-garde graphic design underwent a transformation. It lost its intensity and some of its experimental quality. Nevertheless, corporate patronage has been responsible for much design of high quality and has resulted in recent decades in some of the best American posters. Ivan Chermayeff's inventive poster design for the Mead Paper Company's annual-report competition (plate 210) underscores this fact. The Container Corporation of America was a pioneer in commissioning good designers to do posters, as were Knoll, General Dynamics, Herman Miller, and IBM. However, the purpose of most of these campaigns was to enhance the image of the corporation rather than sell specific products.

While the influence of the Swiss was substantial, particularly

for corporate design programs, American graphic designers took their inspiration from a number of other sources as well. Surrealism and assemblage in various forms have influenced the work of American designers such as Saul Bass, Chermayeff, Alvin Lustig (figure 37), Rand, and Georges Tscherny.

Among the most inventive and poetic works of the early postwar period are the posters for Olivetti by Giovanni Pintori. His 1947 photographic poster, featuring an abacus with a few flowers randomly attached (plate 207), projects a subtle poetry that set a standard for enlightened postwar corporate advertising in its use of an indirect symbol to project an image of the company. In contrast, the handsome corporate posters done by Bayer for Olivetti in 1953 and by Matter for Knoll in 1957 (plates 206, 208) clearly retain the formal approach of the Bauhaus. In this regard, it is also interesting to contrast Bayer's Olivetti poster with *Film* by Fritz Bühler of 1945 (plate 205), a remarkably early use of enlarged duotone photography, displaying a pattern of dots. Here one may see the first indications of the impending shift from a mechanistic to an electronic sensibility.

Figure 35. Raymond Savignac. *L'Eau qui Fait Pschitt.* 1950. Offset lithograph, 90¼ × 63¾″. The Museum of Modern Art, New York. Gift of the designer

Figure 36. Paul Rand. *Subway Posters Score.* 1947. Offset lithograph, 46¼ × 29⅜″. The Museum of Modern Art, New York. Gift of the designer

The new lyrical abstraction produced some extremely interesting typographic work, as in a 1950 poster for Olivetti by Pintori and an exhibition poster by Winfred Gaul of 1960 (plates 215, 216), with overall random arrangements of different sized numbers and calligraphy. Fascinating equivalents are found in Japan in the work of Ryuichi Yamashiro, such as *Forest Wood* (where the Japanese symbol for a tree is repeated to create a forest) of 1954, or the colorful poster by Ikko Tanaka, *Kanze Noh Play*, of 1961 (plates 217, 218). Equally, Bruno Munari's *Campari* poster, a typographic collage (plate 214), can be said to share this sensibility. It is interesting to contrast this with Huber's early work *7 CIAM* (plate 212), with its rigorous Bauhaus-inspired layout. Nevertheless, by his use of bright colors Huber has given this work a light spirit much closer to that of his contemporaries.

Increasingly mannered experimentation in typographic poster design emerged in the mid-1960s. Positive-negative transformations using dot-matrix patterns, the deconstruction of titles, or their metamorphoses from mechanically set type into rough calligraphy, all produced fascinating results. While a number of these manifestations grew out of formal typographic exercises and were mostly done by designers trained in Swiss graphics, it is of interest that this slightly hallucinatory typographic sensibility came into the public arena almost at the same time as the counterculture movement of the mid-1960s.

The search for three-dimensional effects, rendered, in the case of Massimo Vignelli's poster for the thirty-second Venice Biennale, or real, as in Emilio Ambasz's *Geigy Graphics* poster (plates 222, 223), was another aspect of the effort to extend the formal range of typographic design. A. G. Fronzoni's poster *Fontana, Galleria La Polena*, for an artist whose specialty was slitting his canvases, achieved a striking effect with its text printed as if it had been split in the middle (plate 224).

Two posters that summarize another aspect of the 1950s and early 1960s are Pieter Brattinga's *PTT* (plate 234) and Frieder and Renata Grindler's *Kaspar* (plate 235). They beautifully capture the sense of anonymity of a period that seemed to be dominated by corporate culture. In other ways the Grindlers' poster anticipates the new psychedelic sensibility.

The counterculture movement of the mid-1960s was one of the few popular movements to generate its own visual style, the psychedelic poster. The inspiration for this art was diverse, but basic to it was the synergistic combination of rock music and hallucinogenic drugs. More formal visual inspiration came from the rediscovery of Art Nouveau and Viennese

Figure 37. Alvin Lustig and Jay Connor. Design for the cover of *Three Tragedies* by García Lorca. New York: New Directions, 1949. 8½ × 6″. Collection Elaine Lustig Cohen

Secession posters as well as from the contemporary Op art movement. Starting modestly with the San Francisco rock impresario Bill Graham, who commissioned unknown local artists and designers to do posters advertising his concerts, the elements of the style were first crystallized by Robert Wesley Wilson (plate 240). While many contributed to the vitality of the movement, Victor Moscoso was master of the genre, bringing to it a technique, skill, and formal inventiveness that still dazzles (plates 239, 242–245, 247). Ironically, although he is known principally for his work in psychedelic rock posters, Moscoso was not a Haight-Ashbury autodidact. He had studied at Yale with Albers, whose famous Bauhaus-inspired color course, among other things, taught students how to achieve vibrating effects with different colors. While Op art, which also came out of these courses, and emerging computer graphics shared the staccato visual effects of the psychedelic poster, they differed in being essentially impersonal. Nevertheless, the psychedelic poster influenced corporate graphics and the design profession in general.

The Pop art aesthetic came from the everyday world of commercial art and artifacts of consumer culture. Claes Oldenburg transformed ordinary objects into soft or colossal sculptures, or both; Roy Lichtenstein appropriated a cartoon rendering style for his paintings; and James Rosenquist painted billboard-size montages of consumer objects. Andy Warhol was both the most obvious and the most oblique of these artists, appropriating commercial objects directly, on the one hand, or mirroring mass-media photographic images in silkscreen prints, on the other. The transformation of commercial art to high art was applauded by an audience that seemed both attracted by and repelled by consumerism. At another time or place Warhol (who spent his early career in commercial art) might have rendered soup cans as advertisements for the Campbell Soup Company and perhaps been applauded as a worthy successor to Lucian Bernhard. But in the complex art climate of the 1960s in America the deadpan rendering of *Campbell's Tomato Soup* became first an icon of consumer culture, and second, an advertisement, not for soup but for an exhibition of the work of Warhol (plate 254).

Pop art evinced some of the ironic and sometimes cynical stance of Dada, and it was not a coincidence that the work of Marcel Duchamp was rediscovered at the time. Warhol also had the ability to select icons and serve them back to his audience loaded with associations. The pig painted with flowers used in a poster for a color scanner is a case in point (plate 256). In 1968 pigs were often equated with repressive police, but a pig painted with flowers provided associations with the flower children of Haight-Ashbury as well as the decorated piggy bank of childhood.

While Pop art drew heavily on commercial art for its iconography and technique, it, in turn, influenced commercial art. The poster *7 Up*, designed by Robert Abel in 1975 (plate 259), is blatantly commercial in a manner celebrated by Pop art, which it consciously mimics.

The exuberance of the late 1960s had a flip side in serious concerns regarding, among other things, revolution in Latin America and the war in Vietnam. American confidence is captured in a 1963 poster for *Life* magazine by Dennis Wheeler which suggests in a subtle fashion that Castro is about to topple (plate 264). Events, of course, took a different turn, and some years later it seemed that the Cuban revolution, conspicuously symbolized by Che Guevara, might spread all over Latin America (plate 263). The final blow to America's self-image was dealt by the Vietnam war. The posters *End Bad Breath* by Seymour Chwast and *Send Our Boys Home* by Cristos Gianakos suggest both its humbling effect and its tragedy (plates 265, 266).

In Poland, the theater, the circus, and other cultural institu-

tions have become important patrons of artists and the poster has been a prime vehicle for fine artists to achieve national and international recognition. Surrealism and an art of the macabre are the principal and most durable traditions running through this work, which, since its emergence in the 1950s, has produced many memorable and haunting images (plates 267–274).

The Japanese, having been a major influence on the poster medium through their own prints, many of which were, in fact, used as advertising posters in the nineteenth century, have again emerged as a major force in poster design. Japanese designers adopted a modern Constructivist-influenced mode for commercial posters as early as the 1930s. After the Second World War, designers such as Yusaku Kamekura and Ikko Tanaka set a high standard in graphic design that continues to this day. While both have been international in orientation, Tanaka has sought to reconcile modernism with more traditional Japanese motifs, as did Ryuichi Yamashiro.

The emergence of Tadanori Yokoo to prominence in the mid-1960s in Japan marked the arrival of a distinctive talent in graphics that coincided with the counterculture movement and Pop art. Like the psychedelic poster designers and the Pop artists Yokoo has an eclectic approach. The sources for and influences on his work are numerous: he draws on comics, commercial art, Japanese prints, and Western and Oriental religious art for inspiration, combining them in unexpected ways in his posters (plates 275–279).

The Japanese have brought color offset lithographic printing to new heights of refinement and technical skill. This is apparent not only in Yokoo's work but also in the work of Koichi Sato where remarkably subtle color gradations have been achieved (plates 281, 297). This is also true of photographic posters such as the soft-focus nudes of Masatoshi Toda for the Parco department store or Takao Sasai for a beauty contest for hands, *Handle Me*, both of which exhibit a smooth and sensual rendition of skin (plates 283, 284).

The best German work of the 1970s and 1980s has followed a different tradition from that of the Bauhaus with its emphasis on typography, abstraction, and formal composition. Rather, designers such as Günther Kieser, Uwe Loesch, and Gunter Rambow, all of whom studied at the influential school of applied arts in Kassel, are closest to the tradition of Berlin Dada and, in particular, to the work of John Heartfield. Photography is their favored medium, which they use in various ways from a straight photograph of a staged situation to photomontage to manipulations of the photographic image. Although Rambow's *Utopie Dynamit* (plate 291) is an advertisement for a literary publication and not a call for corporate demolition, it has the strident quality of a Heartfield. Kieser's poster *Der stillgelegte Mensch* at first appears as a straightforward photograph of a man, his face covered with pasted-on pills and wearing an appropriately silly smile. In fact, the figure is a constructed doll (plate 286). Loesch's *Punktum* (plate 287), with its close-up of part of a woman's face with a brown mark, sets up a fascinating ambiguity: Is it a beauty mark or a cigarette burn?

The poster by the Swiss designer Christoff Martin Hofstetter for an exhibition of work by artists exiled from Germany in the 1930s is in the same genre, with its evocative view of a gallery wall from which artists' work has been removed (plate 288). The group in the Social Realist painting that remains on the wall conveys a mood of sadness, as if they were mourning the exile of the artists in question. In an ironic juxtaposition, Helmut Schmidt-Rhen's 1978 poster for an exhibition of work by American Neo-Realist painters features a Richard Estes painting partly obscured by a milky film overlay, with the poster text void in the film. This not only plays with the reflective transparencies of Estes's painting but turns the Neo-Realist painting into a highly abstract composition (plate 289).

If the psychedelic poster represented a spontaneous popular revolt against modernist design, and Pop art a similar revolt by artists, the work of Wolfgang Weingart and a number of his former students, among them April Greiman, represents a revolt of a similar nature within the graphic-design establishment itself. Weingart, a German who studied at Basel and stayed on to teach with Hofmann, managed the delicate task of turning most of the unwritten rules of modern Swiss graphics on their heads in his own work while teaching in its inner sanctum. Simplicity, order, clarity, and legibility—all hallmarks of the best Swiss design—have been replaced with a visual complexity that requires detailed attention. Like Dada, one of the aims of his work has been to challenge and subvert a well-established tradition. Assemblages of complex overlapping film patterns, grids, calligraphy, scribbles, and photographs are the elements of Weingart's work. Only the neat typeset titles seem to still indicate the work has come out of the Swiss tradition. Weingart's poster for the exhibition *Das Schweizer Plakat*, perhaps his best-known work (plate 296), is fascinating in another respect. By means of shifting, abstract film patterns and jagged lines he conjures up the Swiss mountain landscape, suggesting that the poster may be an homage to

Herbert Matter's famous work *Für schöne Autofahrten die Schweiz* (plate 179). Greiman, who has also drawn inspiration from Russian Constructivism, has most recently been designing with a computer (plate 298).

However, the modern graphic tradition in Switzerland has retained more vitality than its critics have acknowledged. Niklaus Troxler is one designer who, drawing upon its typographic traditions, has given it a new energy. A jazz enthusiast, Troxler started a successful jazz festival in Mohren for which he has designed numerous posters. In his *McCoy Tyner Sextet* and *A Tribute to the Music of Thelonious Monk* (plates 294, 295), Troxler expressed the staccato rhythms and the mood of the performance in what are essentially purely typographic posters. Like Wilhelm Wenk's 1925 poster *Ein neues Tellenspiel* (plate 118), in which the type suggests the image of a crossbow, Troxler's poster outlines the profile of Monk with the text itself. By varying the colors of the letters, he animates the silhouette and evokes the murky lighting of the performance.

Social and environmental organizations have become major clients of poster designers in recent times. Peace, nuclear war, hunger, and environmental issues have all become topics that have inspired designers to numerous excellent and provocative posters. Among the most poignant is a work by Yusaku Kamekura, *Hiroshima Appeals* (plate 290), with burning butterflies raining down from the sky. The delicacy of the colors belies the horror of the scene. Two of the starkest and most powerful posters of this genre are by Jukka Veistola of Finland: one focusing on world hunger for UNICEF (plate 292) that features an empty plate with a mass of spoons crowding around it, the other (with Tapio Salmelainen) protesting the use of DDT, with a bird wearing a gas mask and singing "DiDiTyy!" (plate 293). The macabre humor of the latter makes the point all too clearly.

It is ironic, but also a sign of vitality, that at the present moment, with printing technology and computer capabilities of unprecedented sophistication at their disposal, a number of graphic designers from different countries are going back to the very beginnings of typography and illustration for inspiration, to graffiti and the primitive scribble of the hand. The poster *On Y Va* by the design group Grapus (plate 301), advertising a festival in Ivry sponsored by the French communist youth movement, is a fascinating example. Growing partly out of the tradition of French protest posters of the late 1960s, it cultivates a spontaneous look achieved by the immediate impact of the slogan *On Y Va*, a standard expression, and by the scribbled subtext added to it, which augments the message and allows a double reading. The first is ostensibly the purpose of the poster: "Let's Go—Everybody to Ivry, to the Party." The other is clearly a political message: "Let's Go—Toward Change."

Throughout its century-long history the poster has proved to be a remarkably resilient medium, adapting itself to a variety of aesthetics and uses. While no longer the principal vehicle for commercial advertising (having been replaced by the illustrated press, radio, and television), it remains important commercially in several contexts, most notably in public environments such as bus, railroad, and subway stations, college campuses, and also along highways in the form of the billboard.

In general, the aesthetic vitality of the commercial poster has declined, although occasionally a corporation commissions a campaign that surprises. But rather than deplore, as many have done, the imminent demise of the poster medium one must separate its commercial function from its other roles. The poster's commercial use has always been only one of its aspects. It is equally significant as a reproducible popular cultural medium that can be used by all—from large institutions to small cultural or political movements and individuals—to give visual expression to their ideas and beliefs. That cannot be said of television, radio, or the press.

Its unique position at the intersection of different artistic mediums; fine and applied arts; handicrafts and mass production; culture, politics, and commerce; and, not least of all, artist and mass audience has brought many of the most ambitious and visionary artists, architects, and designers of the twentieth century to the medium. They have seen the poster as a vehicle for getting out into the streets, beyond the salons and the museums, and engaging the world. Involved in everyday cultural, political, or commercial issues, the poster at its best has been, and continues to be, an extraordinary social and artistic document.

N O T E S

1. Guillaume Apollinaire, "Zone," *Les Soirées de Paris* (December 1912); reprinted in *Oeuvres Complètes de Guillaume Apollinaire*. Paris: André Balland et Jacques Lecat, 1966, p. 55.
2. The Museum of Modern Art first focused on the poster medium in its 1933 *Typography Competition: 20 Best Posters Submitted by American Printers for Museum Use*. The entries were acquired by the Museum at that time but later deaccessioned. In 1935 twenty-six posters (24 by A. M. Cassandre, 1 by Christa Ehrlich) entered the permanent collection.
3. *A New Art Museum*, a brochure issued by the Museum's founders in 1929, quoted in Alfred H. Barr, Jr., "Chronicle of the Collection," in *Painting and Sculpture in The Museum of Modern Art, 1929–1967*. New York: The Museum of Modern Art, 1977, p. 620.
4. Filippo Tommaso Marinetti, *Manifesto of Futurism* (February 20, 1909), in R. W. Flint (ed.), *Marinetti: Selected Writings*. New York: Farrar, Straus and Giroux, 1971, p. 42. First published in *Le Figaro* (Paris), February 24, 1909.
5. *Ibid.*, p. 42.
6. A. Conger Goodyear, "The Directors '1929' Plan," *The Museum of Modern Art: The First Ten Years*. New York, 1943, Appendix A, pp. 137–139.
7. Marinetti, *op. cit.*, p. 42.
8. El Lissitzky, quoted in Herbert Spencer, *Pioneers of Modern Typography*. New York: Hastings House, 1970, p. 1.
9. El Lissitzky, "Our Book,"*Gutenburg-Jahrbuch* (Mainz), 1926–27; reprinted in Sophie Lissitzky-Küppers, *El Lissitzky: Life, Letters, Texts*. Greenwich, Conn.: New York Graphic Society Ltd., 1968, p. 359.
10. ROSTA is an acronym for *Rossiískoe telegrafnoe agentstvo* (Russian Telegraph Agency).
11. VKhUTEMAS is an acronym for *Vysshie khudozhestvenno-tekhnicheskie masterskie* (Higher Artistic and Technical Studios).

PLATES

Note: In the captions, each poster is identified by a plate number and a title, following the name of the designer. Except for Russian and Japanese posters, the title is given as it appears on the work itself, followed when necessary by an English translation in italics. For some works, additional text appears in italics toward the end of the caption. Dimensions are given in inches or in feet and inches, height preceding width. All posters are in the collection of The Museum of Modern Art, New York, and were acquired by gift or purchase, as indicated. Where it has seemed useful, the purpose of the poster is also given. Additional information on the designers appears in the Index of Illustrations.

JULES CHÉRET

1 Les Girard
1879
Lithograph
22⅝ × 17″
Acquired by exchange
. . . .
Cabaret poster

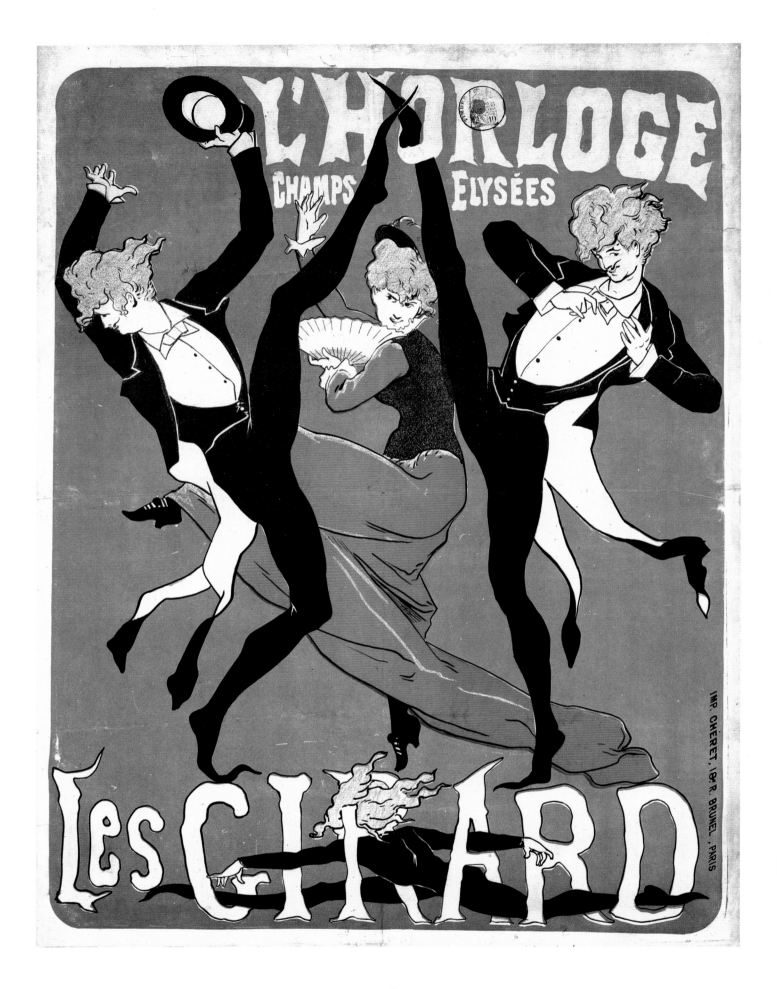

Folies-Bergère, La Loïe Fuller poster

JULES CHÉRET

2 Folies-Bergère, La Loïe Fuller
1893
Lithograph
48½ × 34½″
Acquired by exchange
....
Theater poster

HENRI DE TOULOUSE-LAUTREC

3 Aristide Bruant dans son Cabaret
Aristide Bruant in His Cabaret
1893
Lithograph
53¾ × 37⅞"
Gift of Emilio Sanchez

HENRI DE TOULOUSE-LAUTREC

4 Jane Avril
1893
Lithograph
49⅝ × 36⅛"
Gift of A. Conger Goodyear
. . . .
Cabaret poster

HENRI DE TOULOUSE-LAUTREC

5 Divan Japonais
1893
Lithograph
31⅞ × 24½"
Abby Aldrich Rockefeller Fund
....
Cabaret poster

PIERRE BONNARD

6 France-Champagne

1891

Lithograph

30⅛ × 23″

Purchase fund

. . . .

Advertisement for champagne

PIERRE BONNARD

7 Les Peintres Graveurs

The Painter-Engravers

1896

Lithograph

25½ × 18⅞″

Purchase fund

. . . .

Exhibition poster

PIERRE BONNARD

8 La Revue Blanche

1894

Lithograph

31¾ × 24⅜″

Abby Aldrich Rockefeller Fund

. . . .

Poster for a magazine

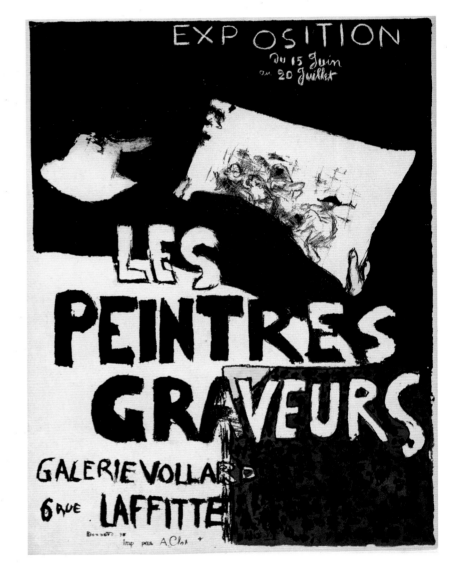

ALPHONSE MUCHA

10 **XXme Exposition du Salon des Cent**
1896
Lithograph
25¼ × 17"
Gift of Ludwig Charell
· · · · · · · · · · · · ·
Exhibition poster

MANUEL ORAZI

11 **Théâtre de Loie Fuller,**
Exposition Universelle
1900
Lithograph
78½ × 25¼"
Gift of Joseph H. Heil
· · · · · · · · · · · · ·
Theater poster

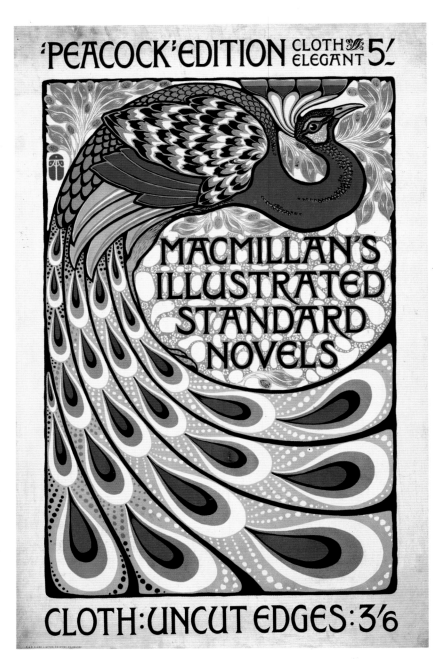

A. A. TURBAYNE

12 Macmillan's Illustrated
Standard Novels
1896
Lithograph
34⅝ × 22½"
Acquired by exchange

AUBREY BEARDSLEY

13 Avenue Theatre, A Comedy
of Sighs!
1894
Lithograph and letterpress
29½ × 19¾"
Acquired by exchange

CHARLES RENNIE MACKINTOSH

14 The Scottish Musical Review
1896
Lithograph
97 × 39"
Acquired by exchange

THE BEGGARSTAFFS: WILLIAM
NICHOLSON AND JAMES PRYDE

15 Rowntree's Elect Cocoa
1895
Lithograph
38 × 28⅝"
Gift of Mr. and Mrs.
Arthur A. Cohen

THE BEGGARSTAFFS: WILLIAM
NICHOLSON AND JAMES PRYDE

16 The Black and White Gallery,
Louis Meyer
c. 1901
Collotype
19 × 26"
Don Page Fund
. . . .
Advertisement for an art gallery

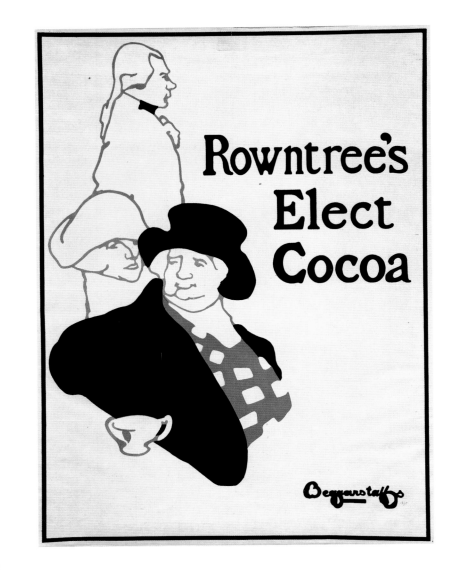

HAMLET.

THE BEGGARSTAFFS: WILLIAM
NICHOLSON AND JAMES PRYDE

17 Hamlet.
   1894
   Stencil
   67⅜ × 28⅞″
   Gift of The Lauder Foundation,
   Leonard and Evelyn Lauder Fund,
   Jack Banning, and by exchange

WILL BRADLEY

18 The Chap Book
1895
Line block
21¼ × 14″
Acquired by exchange
. . . .
Poster for a magazine

WILL BRADLEY

19 The Chap-Book
1895
Lithograph
22 × 15¹⁵⁄₁₆″
Acquired by exchange
. . . .
Poster for a magazine

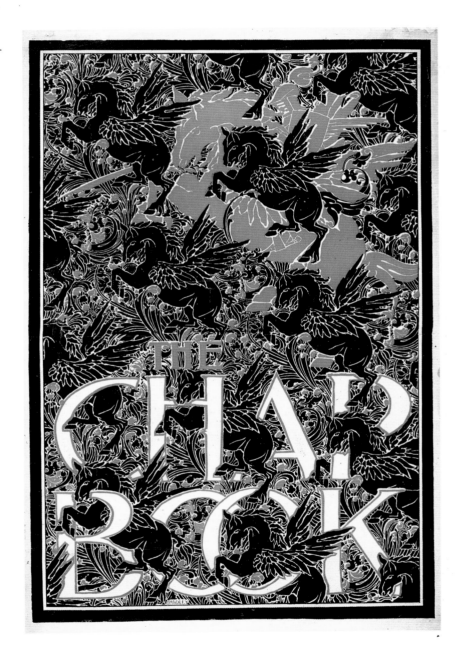

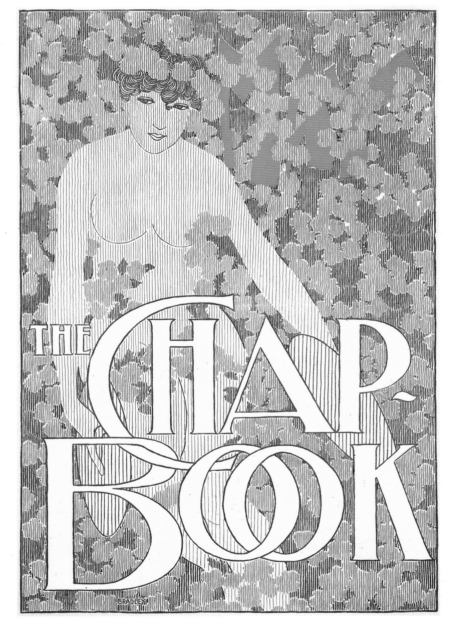

WILL BRADLEY

20 Victor Bicycles
c. 1895
Lithograph
27 × 40⅝"
Gift of The Metropolitan Museum of Art in honor of Leonard A. Lauder

FRANK HAZENPLUG

21 The Chap-Book
   1895
   Lithograph
   21¼ × 13¾″
   Acquired by exchange
   ··············
   Poster for a magazine

EDWARD PENFIELD

22 Harper's March
   1897
   Lithograph
   14 × 19″
   Gift of Poster Originals

DESIGNER UNKNOWN

23 Victor Cycles
1898
Lithograph
28½ × 19⅝"
Gift of The Lauder Foundation

JAMES ENSOR

24 Salon des Cent, James Ensor
1898
Lithograph
25⁹⁄₁₆ × 17¹¹⁄₁₆"
Gift of Ludwig Charell
. . . .
Exhibition poster

JAN TOOROP

25 Delftsche Slaolie
Delft Salad Oil
1895
Lithograph
36½ × 24⅛"
Acquired by exchange

JAN TOOROP

26 Het Hoogeland Beekbergen
1896
Lithograph
36¾ × 27″
Given anonymously
··············
Poster for Het Hoogeland
psychiatric institute

CARLOS SCHWABE

27 Salon Rose + Croix
1892
Lithograph
78 × 31¾″
Given anonymously
············
Exhibition poster

JOHANNES SLUYTERS

28 Zegepraal
Victory
1904
Lithograph
45¾ × 25⅞″
Gift of The Lauder Foundation,
Leonard and Evelyn Lauder Fund
· · · · · · · · · · · ·
Poster for a novel

J. J. CHRISTIAN LEBEAU

29 De Magiër
The Wizard
c. 1914
Lithograph
50⁵⁄₁₆ × 35⅛″
Acquired by exchange
· · · · · · · · · · · ·
Theater poster

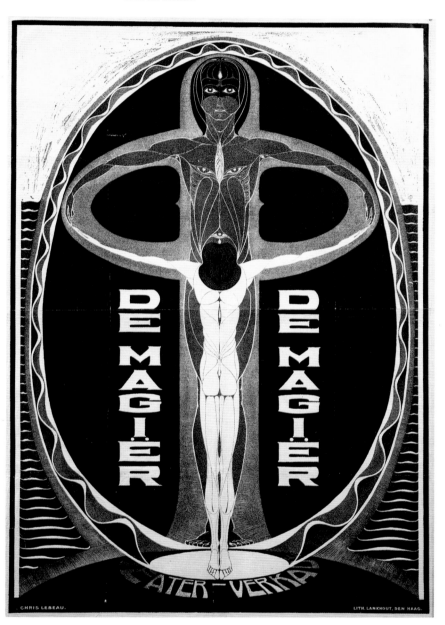

30 Simplicissimus
1897
Lithograph
30 × 20½"
**Gift of The Lauder Foundation,
Leonard and Evelyn Lauder Fund**
....
Poster for a satirical journal

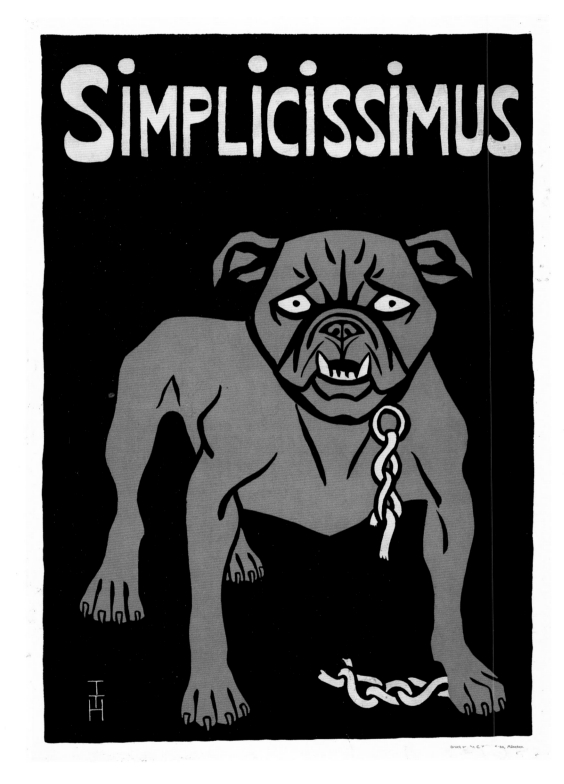

31 **Bil aktie Bol**
 1907
 Lithograph
 34¼ × 45"
 **Purchase fund and gift of Aivi
 and Pirkko Gallen-Kallela**
 . . . .
 Advertisement for an
 automobile company

EMILE PREETORIUS

32 Licht und Schatten
Light and Shadow
1910
Lithograph
11¾ × 8¾"
Gift of The Lauder Foundation,
Leonard and Evelyn Lauder Fund
. . . .
Poster for an art and
poetry magazine

JAN PREISLER

33 Worpswede
1903
Lithograph
31½ × 43½"
Gift of The Lauder Foundation,
Leonard and Evelyn Lauder Fund
. . . .
Exhibition poster

FRITZ BOSCOVITS

34 Bilz Brause
1913
Lithograph
50⅛ × 38½"
Gift of The Lauder Foundation,
Leonard and Evelyn Lauder Fund
· · · · · · · · · · · · ·
Advertisement for a beverage

HENRI MEUNIER

**35 Pollet et Vittet, Chocolaterie
de Pepinster**
c. 1896
Lithograph
19 × 26⅞"
Gift of Joseph H. Heil
· · · · · · · · · · · · ·
Advertisement for cocoa

JOSEF RUDOLF WITZEL

36 Jugend
   1896
   Lithograph
   27⅝ × 45¼"
   Acquired by exchange
   ·············
   Poster for a weekly magazine

HECTOR GUIMARD

37 Exposition Salon du Figaro,
   Le Castel Beranger
   1900
   Lithograph
   35 × 49¼"
   Gift of Lillian Nassau
   ·············
   Exhibition poster

JOHAN THORN-PRIKKER

38 Holländische Kunstausstellung
Dutch Art Exhibition
1903
Lithograph
33⅝ × 47⅞"
**Gift of The Lauder Foundation,
Leonard and Evelyn Lauder Fund**

RICHARD HARLFINGER

39 Secession Plakat Ausstellung
Secession Poster Exhibition
1913
Lithograph
24¾ × 18½"
Acquired by exchange

OTTO MORACH

40 Schweizer Werkbund Ausstellung
Swiss Werkbund Exhibition
1918
Lithograph
47⅜ × 35¹¹⁄₁₆"
Peter Stone Poster Fund

GUSTAV KLIMT

41 1. Kunstausstellung Secession
First Secession Exhibition
1898
Lithograph
25 × 18½"
Gift of Bates Lowry

JOSEPH MARIA OLBRICH

42 Secession
1898
Lithograph
30¾ × 20⅜"
Acquired by exchange
. . . .
Poster for second Secession
exhibition

KOLOMAN MOSER

43 Frommes Kalender
Religious Calendar
1898
Lithograph
37⅜ × 24⅝″
Given anonymously

FERDINAND ANDRI
44 XXV Ausstellung Secession
Twenty-fifth Secession Exhibition
1906
Lithograph
37 × 24½"
**Promised gift of Leonard A.
and Evelyn H. Lauder**

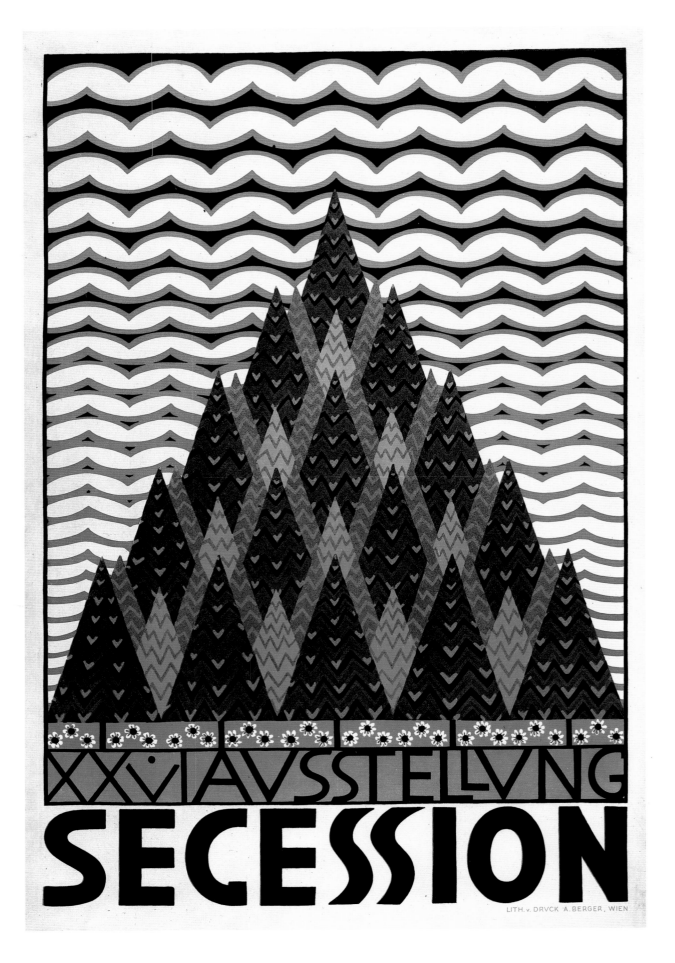

BERTOLD LÖFFLER

45 Kunstschau Wien
Art Show, Vienna
1908
Lithograph
14⅜ × 19½"
**Gift of Leonard A. and
Evelyn H. Lauder**
....
Exhibition poster

OSKAR KOKOSCHKA

46 Kokoschka, Drama-Komoedie
1907
Lithograph
46½ × 30"
Purchase fund
....
Theater poster

MAX OPPENHEIMER

47 Moderne Galerie,
Max Oppenheimer
1911
Lithograph
48⅜ × 35⅝"
Gift of The Lauder Foundation
....
Exhibition poster

EGON SCHIELE

48 Secession 49. Ausstellung
Forty-ninth Secession Exhibition
1918
Lithograph
26¾ × 20⅞"
Gift of Dr. and Mrs. Otto Kallir

FERDINAND HODLER

49 Sechste Ausstellung der
Gesellschaft Schweizer. Maler,
Bildhauer u. Architekten
*Sixth Exhibition of the Swiss Society
of Painters, Sculptors, and
Architects*
1915
Lithograph
39⅝ × 27½"
Purchase fund

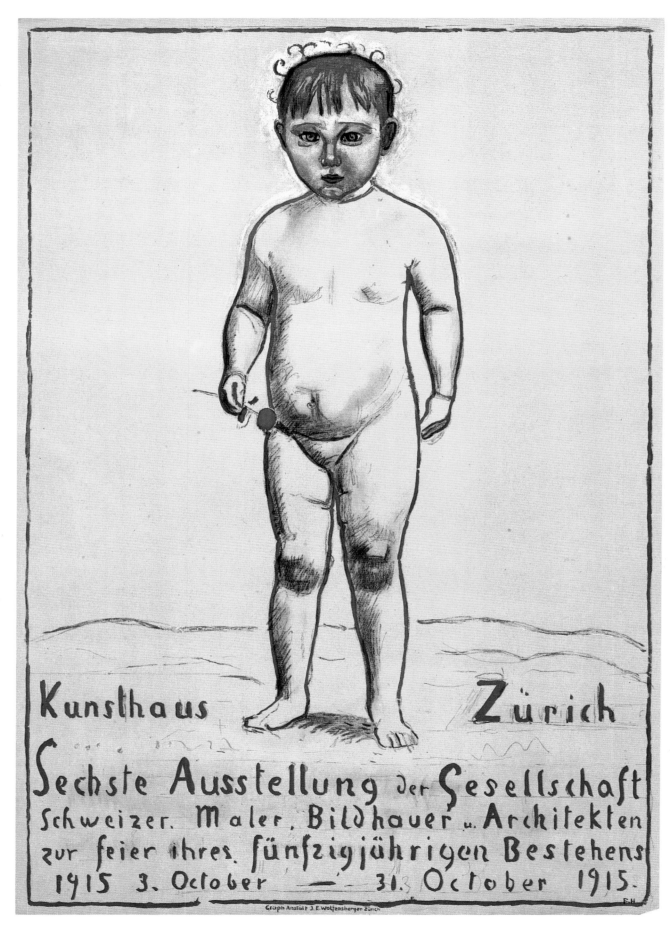

EDUARD RENGGLI

50 56. Eidgenössisches Turnfest in Basel
Fifty-sixth National Gymnastics Festival in Basel
1912
Lithograph
40 × 28¼"
Gift of The Lauder Foundation, Leonard and Evelyn Lauder Fund

LUDWIG HOHLWEIN

51 Starnberger-See
Lake Starnberg
1910
Lithograph
36½ × 49½"
Marshall Cogan Purchase Fund
and by exchange
. . . .
Travel poster

EMILE CARDINAUX

52 Zermatt
1908
Lithograph
40¾ × 28½″
Given anonymously
. . . .
Travel poster

LUDWIG HOHLWEIN

53 Deutsches Theater
1907
Lithograph
49³⁄₁₆ × 36"
Gift of The Lauder Foundation,
Leonard and Evelyn Lauder Fund
....
Advertisement for a restaurant

54 Damenconfectionshaus
Mayer Sundheimer
1909
Lithograph
49¼ × 35⅞″
Gift of The Lauder Foundation,
Leonard and Evelyn Lauder Fund
· · · · · · · · · · · · ·
Advertisement for a
women's clothing store

55 Wilhelm Mozer
1909
Lithograph
49¼ × 34⅜″
Gift of Peter Müller-Munk
· · · · · · · · · · · · ·
Advertisement for a catering
company

LUDWIG HOHLWEIN

56 Hermann Scherrer. Breechesmaker
   Sporting-Tailor
1911
Lithograph
44¼ × 31½"
Gift of Peter Müller-Munk

LUDWIG HOHLWEIN

57 Hermann Scherrer Sporting and
   Ladies-Tailor
1908
Lithograph
48¼ × 35½"
Gift of Peter Müller-Munk

LUDWIG HOHLWEIN

58 Confection Kehl
   1908
   Lithograph
   48½ × 36⅛"
   Gift of Peter Müller-Munk
   . . . .
   Advertisement for a men's
   clothing store

LUDWIG HOHLWEIN

59 Kaffee Hag
1913
Lithograph
35½ × 23⅝"
Gift of The Lauder Foundation,
Leonard and Evelyn Lauder Fund
. . . .
Advertisement for decaffeinated
coffee

LUDWIG HOHLWEIN

60 Marco-Polo-Tee
1910
Lithograph
30⅞ × 21¾"
Gift of The Lauder Foundation,
Leonard and Evelyn Lauder Fund
. . . .
Advertisement for tea

LUDWIG HOHLWEIN

61 Pelikan Künstler-Farben
Pelikan Artists Paints
c. 1925
Lithograph
21¾ × 16⅞"
Gift of The Lauder Foundation,
Leonard and Evelyn Lauder Fund

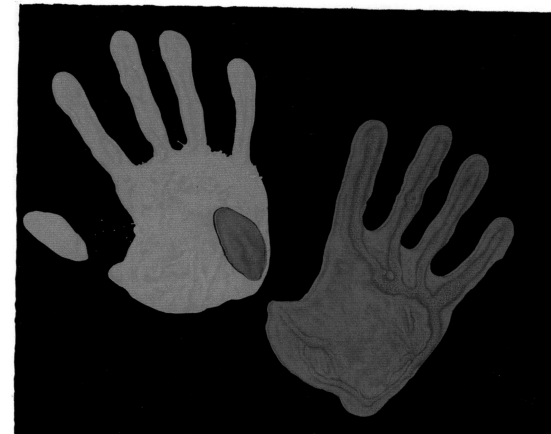
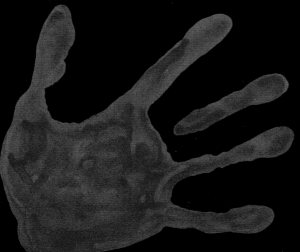

ERNST DEUTSCH

62 Salamander

1912

Lithograph

27¾ × 37⅝"

Gift of The Lauder Foundation, Leonard and Evelyn Lauder Fund

....

Advertisement for shoes

LUCIAN BERNHARD

63 Stiller

1908

Lithograph

27⅛ × 37½"

Gift of The Lauder Foundation, Leonard and Evelyn Lauder Fund

....

Advertisement for a shoe store

LUCIAN BERNHARD

64 Manoli
1910
Lithograph
28 × 37¼″
Don Page Fund
. . . .
Advertisement for cigarettes

JUPP WIERTZ

65 AEG Drahtlampe
AEG Wire Lamp
c. 1915
Lithograph
28¼ × 37¼″
Purchase fund
. . . .
Advertisement for an
electric company

LUCIAN BERNHARD

66 Osram AZO
c. 1910
Lithograph
27⅝ × 37⅜"
Purchase fund
....
Advertisement for light bulbs

LUCIAN BERNHARD

67 Bosch-Licht
   Bosch Light
   1913
   Lithograph
   36¼ × 26¾"
   Gift of The Lauder Foundation,
   Leonard and Evelyn Lauder Fund
   ....
   Advertisement for a lighting
   company

LUCIAN BERNHARD

68 Bosch
1914
Lithograph
17⅞ × 25¼"
Gift of The Lauder Foundation,
Leonard and Evelyn Lauder Fund
. . . .
Advertisement for a lighting
company

LUCIAN BERNHARD

69 Das ist der Weg zum Frieden
That Is the Way to Peace
c. 1917
Lithograph
25¾ × 18⅜"
Gift of Peter Müller-Munk
....
*That Is the Way to Peace—
the Enemies Want It So!
Subscribe to War Loans*

JOHN WARNER NORTON

70 Keep These off the U.S.A.
1918
Lithograph
40⅛ × 30¼"
Acquired by exchange

RUDI SALD

71 Die Gefahr des Bolschewismus
The Danger of Bolshevism
1919
Lithograph
37⅛ × 27⅜″
**Gift of The Lauder Foundation,
Leonard and Evelyn Lauder Fund**

DESIGNER UNKNOWN [A. YU.]

**72 U.S.S.R. Tenth Anniversary.
Our Good Wishes**
1927
Lithograph
39 × 27⅞″
Given anonymously

MAX PECHSTEIN

73 An die Laterne
To the Lamppost
c. 1920
Lithograph
28⅜ × 37⅜″
Gift of The Lauder Foundation,
Leonard and Evelyn Lauder Fund
· · · · · · · · · · · ·
Political poster

HEINZ FUCHS

74 Arbeiter Hunger Tod naht
Worker Starvation Is Approaching
1919
Lithograph
29½ × 40¾″
Gift of Peter Müller-Munk
· · · · · · · · · · · ·
Worker Starvation Is Approaching.
Strike Destroys, Work Nourishes.
Do Your Duty. Work.

LOUIS RAEMAEKERS

75 Tegen de Tariefwet
Antitariff Act
1913
Lithograph
38⅞ × 30½″
Given anonymously
· · · · · · · · · · · ·
Antitariff Act, Don't
Fly into the Web!

94

76 Der Golem: Wie er in die Welt kam
The Golem: As He Came into the
World
1920
Lithograph
28½ × 37"
Gift of Universum Film
Aktiengesellschaft

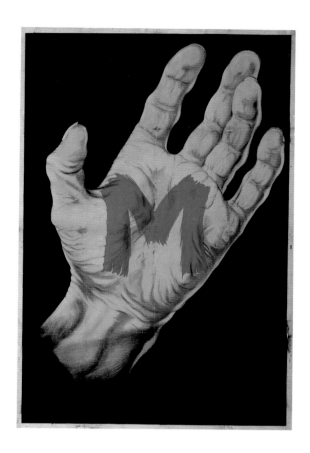

Kurt Wenzel

77 M
   1931
   Lithograph
   56 × 37¼″
   Acquired by exchange
   . . . .
   Film poster

Stahl-Arpke

78 Das Cabinet des Dr. Caligari
   The Cabinet of Dr. Caligari
   1919
   Lithograph
   27⅛ × 37″
   Gift of Universum Film
   Aktiengesellschaft
   . . . .
   Film poster

KARL MICHEL

79 Faust
1927
Lithograph
55¼ × 36½"
Gift of Universum Film
Aktiengesellschaft
. . . .
Film poster

E. McKnight Kauffer

81 Untitled
1919
Lithograph
39¼ × 59⅝"
Gift of the designer
· · · · · · · · · · · · ·
**Top section of a poster
for *The Daily Herald***

E. McKnight Kauffer

82 Winter Sales
1921
Lithograph
39¾ × 24¼"
Gift of the designer
· · · · · · · · · · · · ·
Transportation poster

KAREL MAES

83 De Vertraagde Film
The Slow-Motion Film
1922
Lithograph
42⅛ × 31¼"
Purchase fund
....
Theater poster

THEO VAN DOESBURG
AND KURT SCHWITTERS

84 Kleine Dada Soirée
Small Dada Evening
1922
Lithograph
11⅞ × 11¼"
Gift of Philip Johnson,
Jan Tschichold Collection

Ilia Zdanevitch

85 Iliazde
1922
Lithograph
21⅜ × 19⅛"
Arthur A. Cohen Purchase Fund
....
Exhibition poster

El Lissitzky

86 Merz-Matinéen
Merz Matinee
1923
Letterpress
9 × 11"
Gift of Philip Johnson

Jean Crotti and
Suzanne Duchamp

87 Tabu
1921
Lithograph
47½ × 31½"
Purchase fund
....
Exhibition poster

ROBERT DELAUNAY AND
GRANOVSKY

88 Soirée du Coeur à Barbe
Evening of the Bearded Heart
1923
Lithograph
35⅜ × 23⅝″
Given anonymously
. . . .
Theater poster

MAX ERNST

89 Arp, Max Ernst, A. Giacometti,
Miro, Gonzalez
1934
Letterpress
39 × 27¼″
Gift of Kunsthaus Zurich
. . . .
*An Image Is an Abstract Likeness
Through Imagination*
Exhibition poster

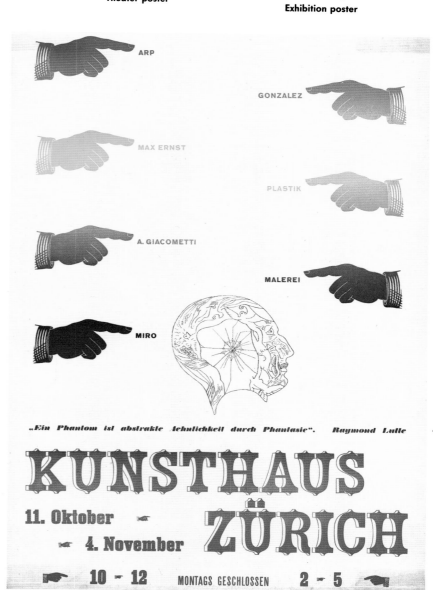

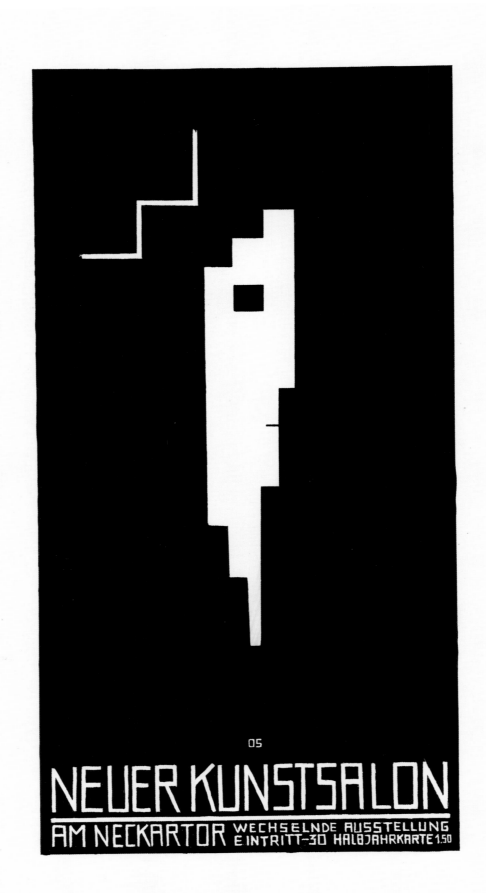

OSKAR SCHLEMMER

90 Neuer Kunstsalon
   New Art Salon
   1913
   Lithograph
   22¾ × 12¾"
   Gift of The Lauder Foundation,
   Leonard and Evelyn Lauder Fund
   . . . .
   Exhibition poster

Joost Schmidt

91 Staatliches Bauhaus Ausstellung
   National Bauhaus Exhibition
   1923
   Lithograph
   26¼ × 18⅝"
   Gift of Walter Gropius

Oskar Schlemmer

92 Grosse Brücken Revue
   Great Bridges Revue
   1926
   Lithograph
   46½ × 36"
   Abby Aldrich Rockefeller Fund,
   Jan Tschichold Collection
   ....
   Great Bridges Revue:
   Pantomime in Three Parts
   Poster for opening ceremony
   of Frankfurt bridge

HERBERT BAYER

93 Architektur Lichtbilder Vortrag,
Professor Hans Poelzig
*Architecture Slide Lecture,
Professor Hans Poelzig*
1926
Letterpress
19⅛ × 25⅝"
Gift of Philip Johnson

WALTER DEXEL

94 Verwende Stets nur Gas
Always Use Gas
1924
Letterpress
19 × 25"
Purchase fund
....
*Always Use Gas for Cooking,
Baking, Heating, Lighting
Because It Is Practical, Clean,
Inexpensive, Saves Work,
Time, Money*

HERBERT BAYER

95 Kandinsky zum 60. Geburtstag
Kandinsky on His Sixtieth Birthday
1926
Offset lithograph
19 × 25"
Gift of Mr. and Mrs. Alfred H. Barr, Jr.
. . . .
Exhibition poster

HERBERT BAYER

96 Ausstellung Europäisches
   Kunstgewerbe
   European Arts and Crafts Exhibition
   1927
   Lithograph
   35¼ × 23¾"
   Gift of Mr. and Mrs. Alfred H. Barr, Jr.

F. H. WENZEL

97 Schau Fenster Schau
   Show Window Show
   1928
   Lithograph
   36½ × 23⁹⁄₁₆"
   Gift of The Lauder Foundation,
   Leonard and Evelyn Lauder Fund
   ·············
   Poster for window-display
   exhibition

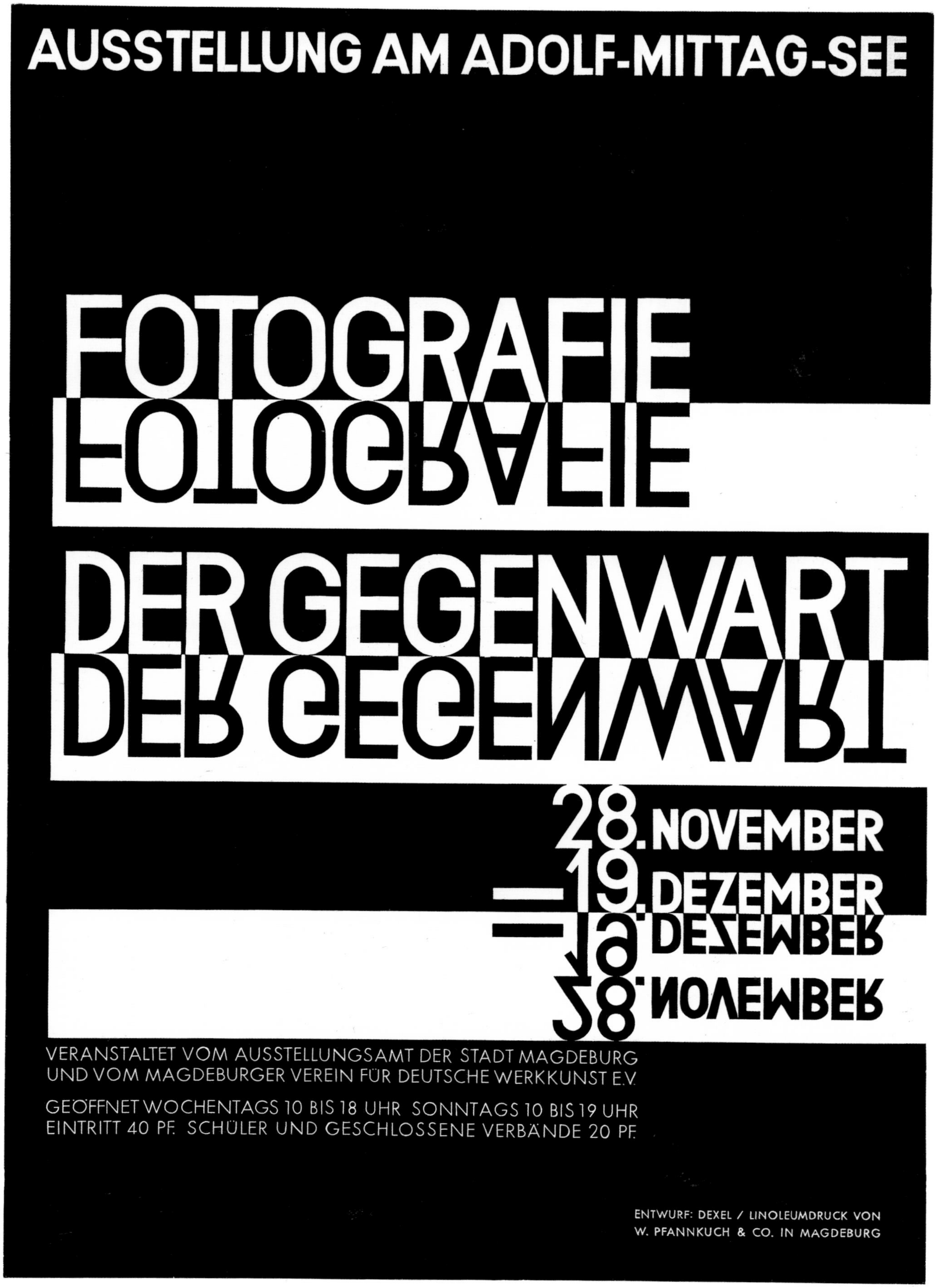

WALTER DEXEL
98 Fotografie der Gegenwart
   Contemporary Photography
   1929
   Linocut
   33⅛ × 23⅜"
   Gift of the designer
   . . . .
   Exhibition poster

JAN TSCHICHOLD

100 Die Frau ohne Namen
The Woman Without Name
1927
Offset lithograph
48¾ × 34"
Peter Stone Poster Fund
. . . .
Film poster

MAX BURCHARTZ

102 Schubertfeier
Schubert Festival
1928
Offset lithograph
23¼ × 33″
Gift of Philip Johnson
. . . .
Concert poster

103 **Wie Wohnen? Die Wohnung**
Werkbund Ausstellung
How to Live? The Dwelling
Werkbund Exhibition
1927
Offset lithograph
44¾ × 32⅜"
Gift of Philip Johnson

HELMUT KURTZ

104 **Ausstellung Neue Haus-Wirtschaft**
Household Design Exhibition
1930
Gravure
50⅜ × 35⅝"
Gift of The Lauder Foundation,
Leonard and Evelyn Lauder Fund

JOHANNES MOLZAHN

105 Wohnung und Werkraum
Dwelling and Work Place
1929
Lithograph
23⅝ × 32¾"
Gift of Philip Johnson,
Jan Tschichold Collection
. . . .
Poster for Werkbund exhibition,
Breslau

JOHANNES MOLZAHN

106 Wohnung und Werkraum
Dwelling and Work Place
1929
Gravure
23¾ × 33"
Purchase fund, Jan Tschichold
Collection
. . . .
Poster for Werkbund exhibition,
Breslau

HERBERT BAYER

HERBERT BAYER

107 IBA

1934

Offset lithograph

46½ × 33⅛"

Given anonymously

. . . .

Poster for international
office exhibition, Berlin

PAUL SCHUITEMA

108 ANVV

1932

Lithograph

11½ × 13⅞"

Acquired by exchange

. . . .

*Buy ANVV Stamps, Support
the Work of the General Dutch
Union for Foreign Travel*

HERBERT BAYER

109 Section Allemande
German Section
1930
Lithograph
15½ × 11¾"
Purchase fund
....
Exhibition poster for society
of decorative artists

110 Batavier-Line Rotterdam London
c. 1915
Lithograph
29⅞ × 44″
Given anonymously
....
Transportation poster

HENDRIKUS WIJDEVELD

**111 Eere Tentoonstelling
Th: Colenbrander**

*Exhibition in Honor of
Th. Colenbrander*

1923

Letterpress

39½ × 22⅞″

**Gift of The Lauder Foundation,
Leonard and Evelyn Lauder Fund**

CHRISTA EHRLICH

**112 Ostenrijksche Schilderijen en
Kunstnijverheid 1900–1927**

*Austrian Paintings and
Industrial Arts 1900–1927*

1927

Linocut

14⁷⁄₁₆ × 14¾″

Gift of Mrs. Alfred H. Barr, Jr.

....

Exhibition poster

Gerard Baksteen

113 **Moderne Kunst**
Modern Art
c. 1930
Lithograph
38¼ × 29"
Gift of The Lauder Foundation, Leonard and Evelyn Lauder Fund
....
Exhibition poster

PIET ZWART

114 ITF
1928
Lithograph
42¼ × 30⅝"
Acquired by exchange
....
Poster for international film
exhibition

THEO H. BALLMER

119 Neues Bauen
New Building
1928
Lithograph
50⅛ × 35⅝"
Gift of The Lauder Foundation
....
Exhibition poster

THEO H. BALLMER

120 Bureau Bâle
1928
Lithograph
50¹⁄₁₆ × 35½"
Estée and Joseph Lauder
Design Fund
....
Poster for international office
design exhibition, Basel

THEO H. BALLMER

121 Büro
1928
Lithograph
50⅛ × 35⅜″
Gift of The Lauder Foundation
·············
Poster for international
office design exhibition

THEO H. BALLMER

122 Norm
1928
Lithograph
49⅞ × 35⅝″
Estée and Joseph Lauder
Design Fund
·············
Poster for exhibition of
industrial design standards

ALEXEY BRODOVITCH

123 Martini
1926
Linocut
46½ × 60⅝"
Gift of Bernard Davis
. . . .
Advertisement for vermouth

OTTO BAUMBERGER

124 Forster Ausverkauf
Forster Sale
1928
Linocut
50⅜ × 35½"
Gift of The Lauder Foundation,
Leonard and Evelyn Lauder Fund
. . . .
Advertisement for a carpet store

JEAN ARP AND WALTER CYLIAX

125 Abstrakte und Surrealistische
Malerei und Plastik
*Abstract and Surrealist
Painting and Sculpture*
1929
Lithograph
50⅜ × 35⅛"
Purchase fund, Jan Tschichold
Collection
. . . .
Exhibition poster

MAX BILL

126 Negerkunst prähistorische
Felsbilder südafrikas
*Negro Art, Prehistoric Rock
Painting of South Africa*
1931
Linocut
50⅛ × 34⅞″
Gift of the designer
. . . .
Exhibition poster

JAN TSCHICHOLD

127 Konstruktivisten
Constructivists
1937
Offset lithograph
50¼ × 35½″
Abby Aldrich Rockefeller Fund,
Jan Tschichold Collection
. . . .
Exhibition poster

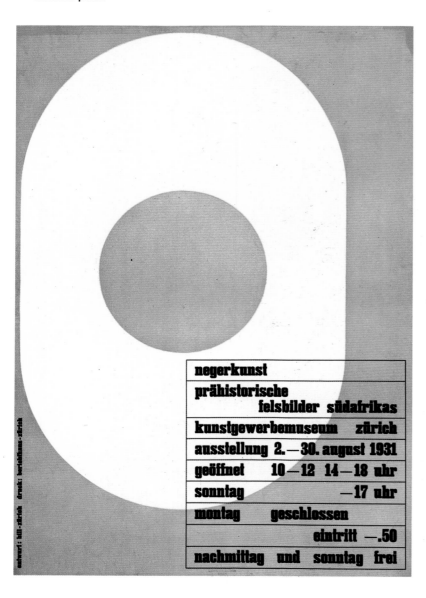

JAN TSCHICHOLD

128 Der Berufsphotograph
The Professional Photographer
1938
Offset lithograph
25⅛ × 35¼″
Gift of the designer
. . . .
Exhibition poster

ALEXANDER RODCHENKO

129 Inga
c. 1929
Letterpress
28¾ × 41¾"
Gift of Jay Leyda
....
*Inga, a Psychological Drama
in Four Acts*
Theater poster

V. SIMOV AND I. STEPANOV

130 The Victory of a Woman
1927
Offset lithograph
27⅝ × 42⅜"
Given anonymously
....
Film poster

DESIGNER UNKNOWN

131 MAKhD

c. 1925

Offset lithograph

42⅜ × 28¼″

Given anonymously

· · · · · · · · · · · · · ·

**Poster for first exhibition
of Moscow association of
artists and decorators**

ALEXEI GAN

**132 First Exhibition of Contemporary
Architects**

1927

Letterpress

42¼ × 27⅝″

Gift of Alfred H. Barr, Jr.

ALEXANDER RODCHENKO

133 Dobrolet
1923
Offset lithograph
13¾ × 17⅞"
Given anonymously
. . . .
To All . . . To All . . . To All . .
He Who Isn't a Stockholder in
Dobrolet Is Not a Citizen of
the USSR

Airline poster

YAKOV GUMINER

134 May First
1923
Offset lithograph
43 × 24"
Given anonymously
. . . .
Political poster

DESIGNER UNKNOWN

135 Fighting Lazy Workers
1931
Offset lithograph
27⅜ × 40⅞"
Gift of Miss Jessie Rosenfeld

ALEXANDER RODCHENKO

136 Film Eye
1924
Lithograph
36½ × 27½″
Gift of Jay Leyda
....
Poster for six films by Dziga Vertov

VLADIMIR AND GEORGII
STENBERG

138 Zvenigora
1927
Offset lithograph
41½ × 27½"
Purchase fund
....
Film poster

KRICHEVSKI

139 Zvenigora
1927
Lithograph
40 × 28"
Given anonymously
....
Film poster

VLADIMIR AND GEORGII
STENBERG

140 Forced Labor
1928
Offset lithograph
48¼ × 27¾"
Given anonymously
....
Film poster

141 The Three-Million Case
1927
Lithograph
28¼ × 42⅜"
Given anonymously
. . . .
Film poster

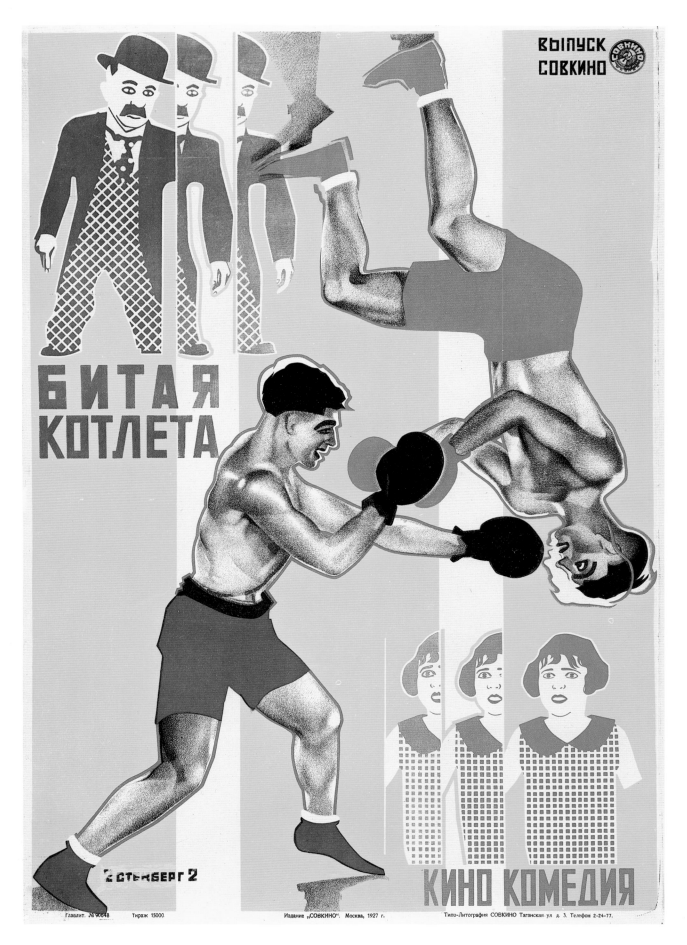

VLADIMIR AND GEORGII
STENBERG

142 Pounded Cutlet
1927
Lithograph
40 × 27½"
Gift of The Lauder Foundation,
Leonard and Evelyn Lauder Fund
....
Film poster

Nikolai Prusakov

143 Pipe of the Communards
1930
Lithograph
42⁹⁄₁₆ × 28⅜″
Poster fund

Film poster

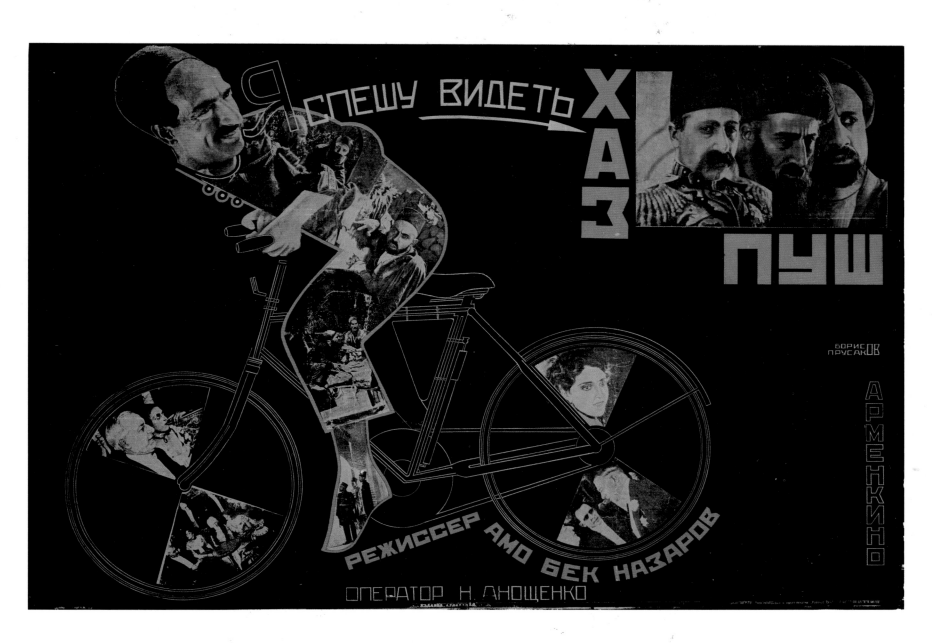

GRIGORY BORISOV AND
NIKOLAI PRUSAKOV

144 I Hurry to See Khaz Push
1927
Offset lithograph
28 × 41½″
Given anonymously
·············
Film poster

ANATOLI BELSKI

145 Pipe of the Communards
1929
Lithograph
43 × 29¼"
Gift of The Lauder Foundation,
Leonard and Evelyn Lauder Fund
....
Film poster

144

YAKOV GUMINER

146 1917
   1927
   Offset lithograph
   41⅞ × 26⅝"
   Gift of Alfred H. Barr, Jr.
   . . . .
   Film poster

GUSTAV KLUTSIS

147 The Development of Transportation,
The Five-Year Plan
1929
Gravure
28⅞ × 19⅞"
Purchase fund, Jan Tschichold
Collection

MICHAEL DOLGORUKOW

148 Transport Worker Arms Himself
with Technical Skill
1931
Offset lithograph
40⅞ × 28¾"
Given anonymously
. . . .
*Transport Worker Arms Himself
with Technical Skill. Strive to
Reconstruct Transportation*

EL LISSITZKY

149 USSR Russische Ausstellung
Russian Exhibition
1929
Gravure
49 × 35¼"
**Gift of Philip Johnson,
Jan Tschichold Collection**

GUSTAV KLUTSIS

150 Onward into the Third Year
1930
Gravure
40½ × 29½″
Purchase fund, Jan Tschichold
Collection
· · · · · · · · · · · · ·
Poster for the five-year plan

GUSTAV KLUTSIS

151 We Will Return Our Coal Debt
to the Country
1930
Gravure
41 × 29⅛″
Purchase fund, Jan Tschichold
Collection

GUSTAV KLUTSIS

152 Fulfilled Plan, Great Work
1930
Gravure
46¾ × 33¼"
Purchase fund, Jan Tschichold
Collection
. . . .
Poster for the five-year plan

A. M. Cassandre

153 La Route Bleue
1929
Lithograph
39⅜ × 24⅜″
Gift of French National Railways
....
Transportation poster

A. M. CASSANDRE

154 Étoile du Nord
1927
Lithograph
41⅜ × 29¾"
Gift of The Lauder Foundation,
Leonard and Evelyn Lauder Fund
....
Transportation poster

A. M. CASSANDRE

155 Nord Express
   1927
   Lithograph
   41 × 29½"
   Gift of French National Railways
   ....
   Transportation poster

A. M. Cassandre

156 L.M.S. Best Way
1928
Lithograph
41⅜ × 50¾"
Gift of The Lauder Foundation
· · · · · · · · · · · · ·
Transportation poster

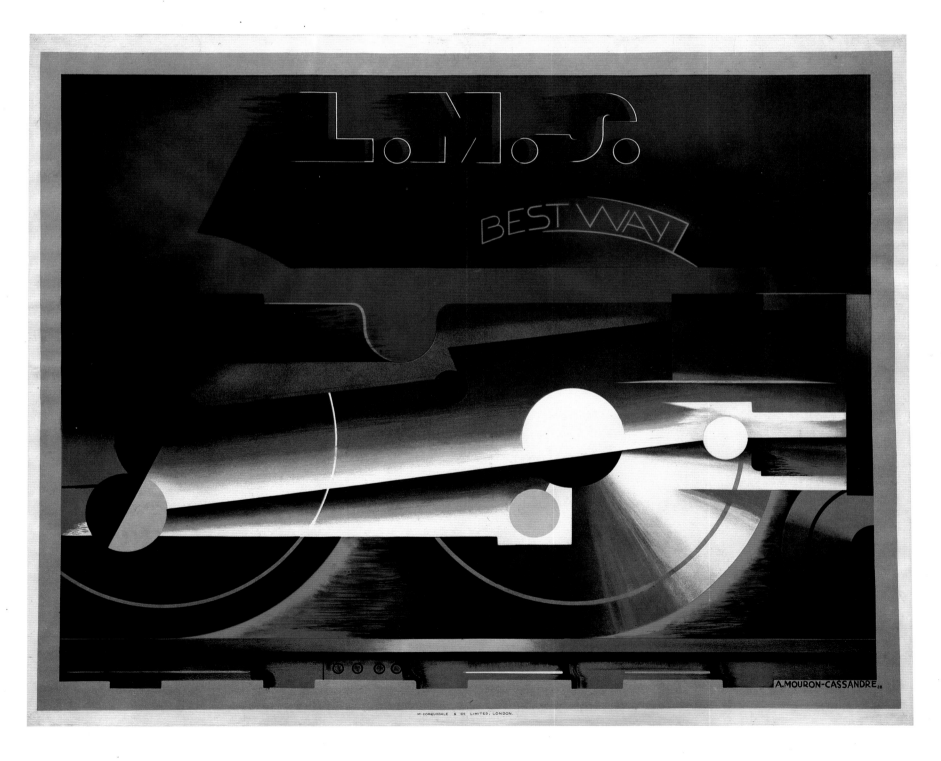

A. M. CASSANDRE

157 Restaurez-vous au Wagon-Bar
1932
Lithograph
39⅜ × 24⅜″
Gift of Benjamin Weiss
....
Transportation poster

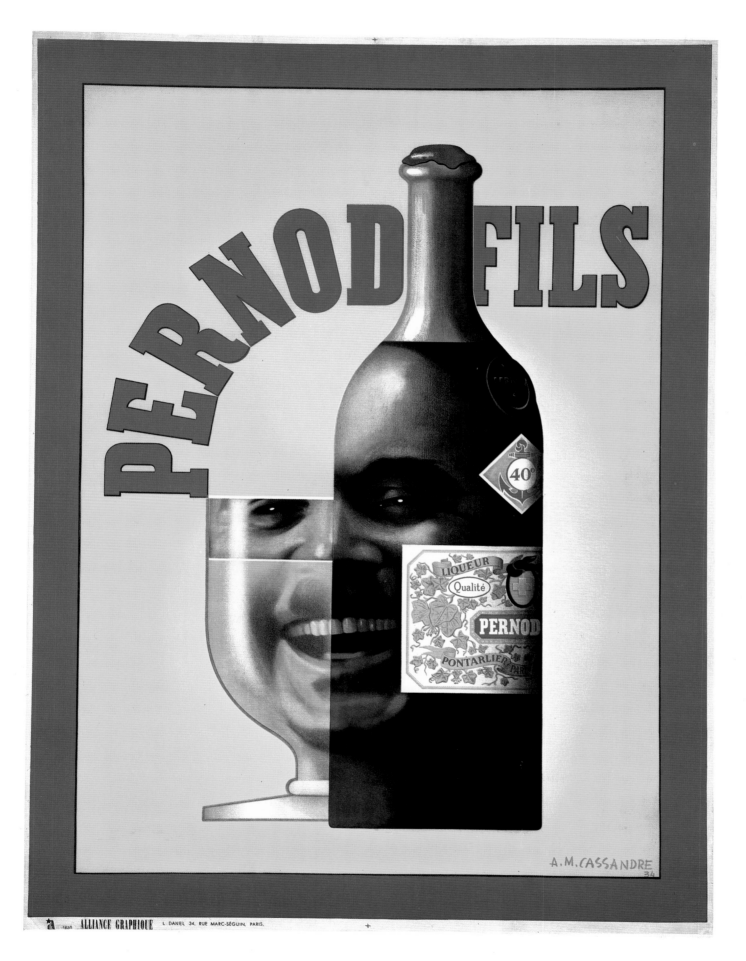

A. M. Cassandre

158 Pernod Fils
    1934
    Lithograph
    63⅛ × 47″
    **Gift of The Lauder Foundation,
    Leonard and Evelyn Lauder Fund**
    . . . .
    Advertisement for an aperitif

A. M. CASSANDRE

159 NEderlandsche NYverheidsten
TOonstelling
Dutch Industrial Exhibition
1928
Lithograph
41⁵⁄₁₆ × 29½″
Given anonymously

A. M. CASSANDRE

160 S.S. "Côte d'Azur"
1931
Lithograph
39 × 24⅝″
Gift of Mr. and Mrs. Stanley Resor
. . . .
Transportation poster

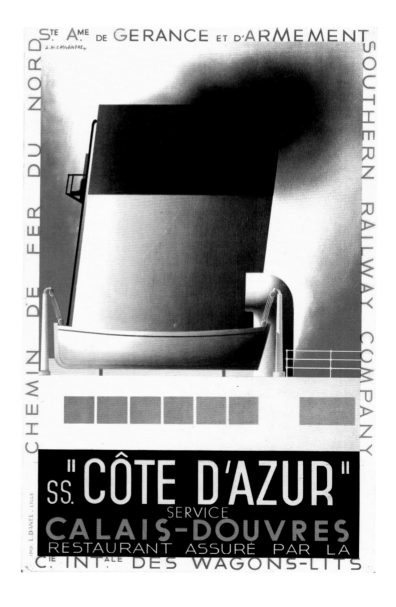

A. M. Cassandre

163 Dubo Dubon Dubonnet

1932

Lithograph

17½ × 45½″

Gift of Bernard Davis

. . . .

Advertisement for an aperitif

E. McKnight Kauffer

164 Magicians Prefer Shell
1934
Lithograph
30 × 45"
Gift of the designer
....
Advertisement for an oil company

E. McKnight Kauffer

165 Metropolis
1926
Tempera
18½ × 29¾"
Given anonymously
· · · · · · · · · · · · ·
Maquette for a film poster

E. McKnight Kauffer

166 Shop Between 10 and 4
1930
Lithograph
39⅜ × 24⅞"
Gift of the designer
· · · · · · · · · · · · ·
Transportation poster

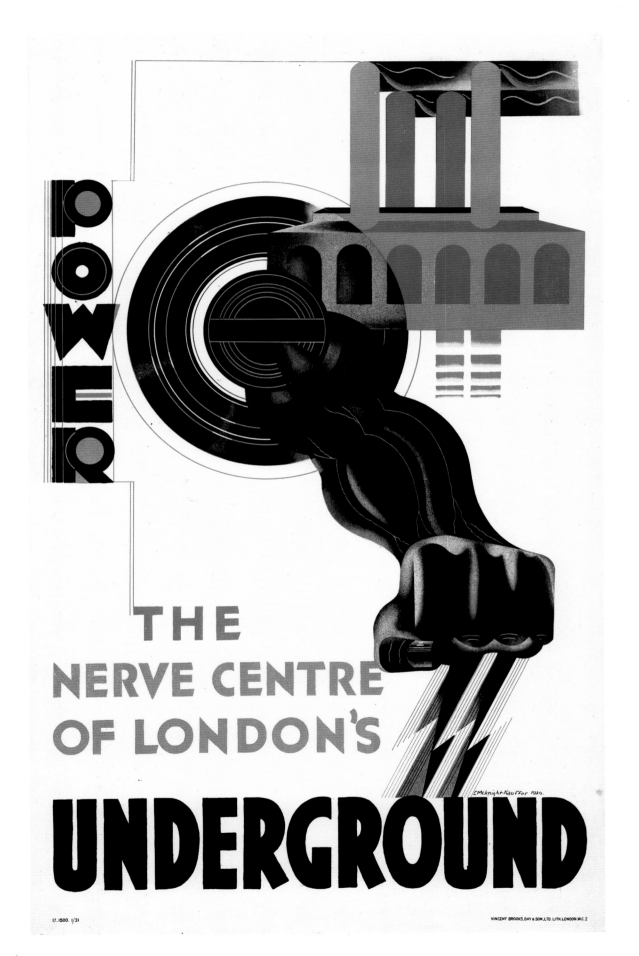

E. McKnight Kauffer

167 Power, the Nerve Centre of
London's Underground
1930
Lithograph
40 × 24¾"
Gift of the designer
....
Transportation poster

Man Ray

168 Keeps London Going
1932
Offset lithograph
39⅝ × 24¼"
Gift of Bernard Davis
....
Transportation poster

A. M. CASSANDRE

169 Watch the Fords Go By
1937
Offset lithograph
8'11" × 19'6½"
Gift of the designer

J. P. Junot

170 Paris Liege
1930
Lithograph
39½ × 24½"
Acquired by exchange
....
Paris to Liege in 4 Hours
367 Kms. Nonstop

Transportation poster

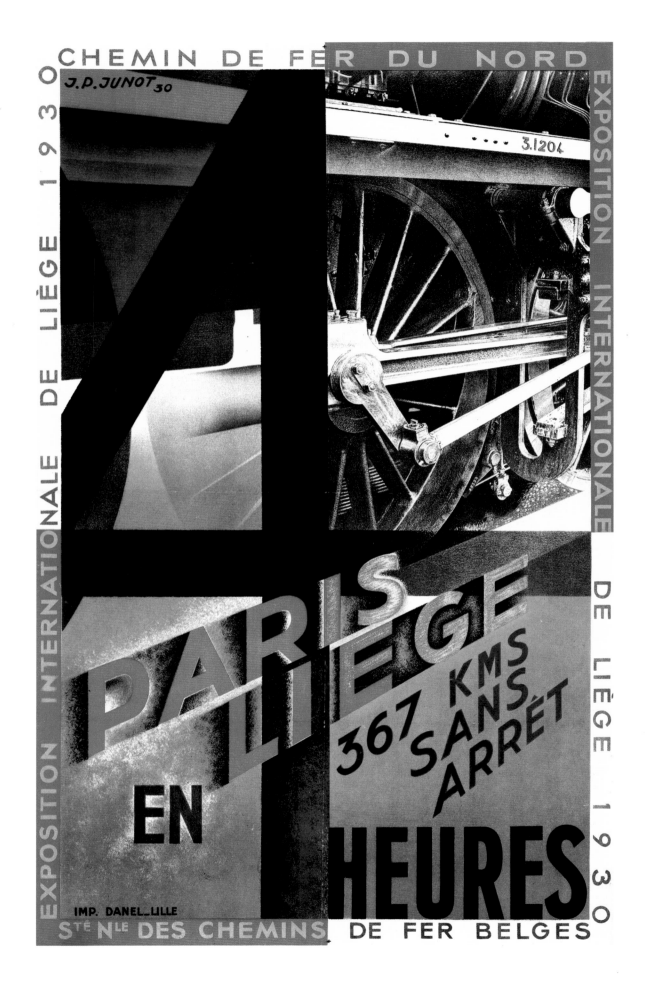

PIERRE FIX-MASSEAU

171 Exactitude
1932
Offset lithograph
39⅜ × 24¼"
Gift of French National Railways
....
Transportation poster

CHARLES LOUPOT

172 Voisin Automobiles
1923
Lithograph
64 × 47¾"
Gift of The Lauder Foundation,
Leonard and Evelyn Lauder Fund

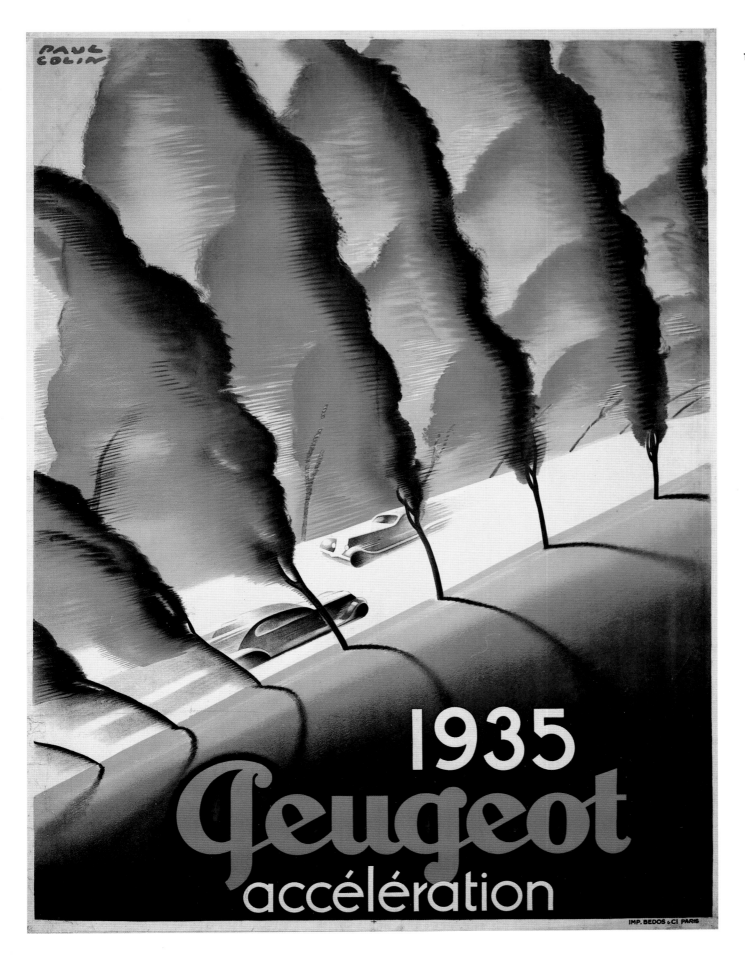

PAUL COLIN

173 Peugeot
1935
Lithograph
63 × 46¾"
Gift of Bernard Davis

U. DI LAZZARO

174 Italian Aerial Lines
 c. 1933
 Lithograph
 39⅜ × 23¹¹/₁₆″
 Purchase fund

MUNETSUGU SATOMI

175 K.L.M.
 1933
 Lithograph
 39¼ × 24⅛″
 Gift of Bernard Davis

176 BMW Motorräder
BMW Motorcycles
c. 1935
Lithograph
39½ × 26"
Purchase fund, Jan Tschichold
Collection

177 Between Your Brakes and
the Road, Goodyear
c. 1932
Offset lithograph
38 × 24"
Gift of The Lauder Foundation,
Leonard and Evelyn Lauder Fund

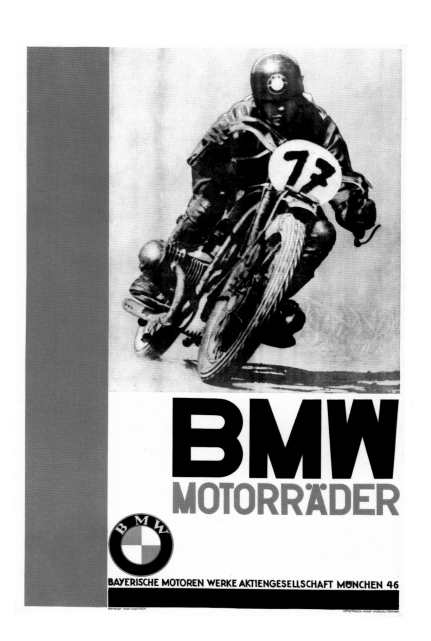

E. McKnight Kauffer

178 Great Western to Devon's Moors
1932
Lithograph
39⅛ × 24"
Gift of the designer
. . . .
Railway poster

Herbert Matter

179 Für schöne Autofahrten die Schweiz
*For Beautiful Automobile Trips,
Switzerland*
1935
Gravure
39¾ × 25⅛"
Gift of Bernard Davis

HERBERT MATTER

180 Pontresina Engadin
1935
Gravure
41 × 25⅛"
Gift of the designer
....
Travel poster

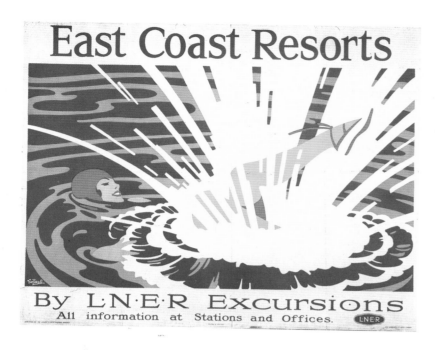

TOM PURVIS

182 East Coast Resorts
    1925
    Lithograph
    39½ × 50″
    Given anonymously
    · · · · · · · · · · · ·
    Transportation poster

TOM PURVIS

183 East Coast by LNER
    c. 1928
    Lithograph
    39¼ × 50″
    Given anonymously
    · · · · · · · · · · · ·
    Transportation poster

FRANCIS BERNARD

184 Gaz Cuit–Chauffe–Glace
Gas, Cook–Heat–Cool
1928
Lithograph
63 × 47¼"
Purchase fund

LESTER BEALL

185 Running Water, Rural Electrification
Administration
1937
Silkscreen
40 × 30"
Gift of the designer

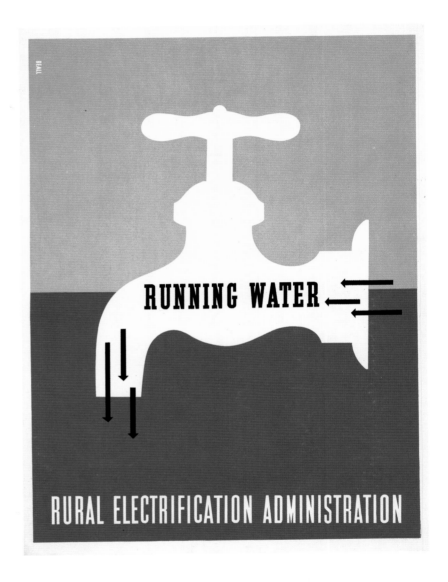

OTTO BAUMBERGER

188 PKZ

1923

Lithograph

50⅛ × 35½"

Estée and Joseph Lauder
Design Fund

. . . .

Advertisement for a men's
clothing store

OTTO BAUMBERGER

189 Baumann
1922
Lithograph
50¼ × 35¾"
Purchase fund
. . . .
Advertisement for a men's
clothing store

PIERRE GAUCHAT

190 Bally
1935
Lithograph
50⅝ × 35½"
Purchase fund, Jan Tschichold
Collection
. . . .
Advertisement for shoes

ALEX W. DIGGELMANN

191 PKZ Burger-Kehl & Co. AG
1935
Lithograph
50½ × 35⅝"
Gift of Emilio Sanchez
. . . .
Advertisement for a men's
clothing store

LUDWIG HOHLWEIN

192 Und Du?

And You?

1929

Offset lithograph

47 × 32¼"

Purchase fund

. . . .

Political poster

VICTOR ANCONA AND

KARL KOEHLER

193 This Is the Enemy

1942

Offset lithograph

34¼ × 23¾"

Poster fund

This is Nazi brutality

RADIO BERLIN.--IT IS OFFICIALLY ANNOUNCED:-
ALL MEN OF LIDICE - CZECHOSLOVAKIA - HAVE BEEN SHOT:
THE WOMEN DEPORTED TO A CONCENTRATION CAMP:
THE CHILDREN SENT TO APPROPRIATE CENTERS-- THE
NAME OF THE VILLAGE WAS IMMEDIATELY ABOLISHED.
6/11/42/115P

BEN SHAHN

194 This Is Nazi Brutality
1943
Offset lithograph
38¼ × 27⅞″
**Gift of the Office of War
Information**

197 America's Answer! Production
1942
Offset lithograph
29⅞ × 39⅝"
Gift of the Office for
Emergency Management

BEN SHAHN

198 Break Reaction's Grip,
Register, Vote
1944
Offset lithograph
41⅝ × 29″
Gift of S. S. Spivack

HERBERT BAYER

199 Polio Research
1949
Offset lithograph
44½ × 29″
Gift of Infantile
Paralysis Foundation

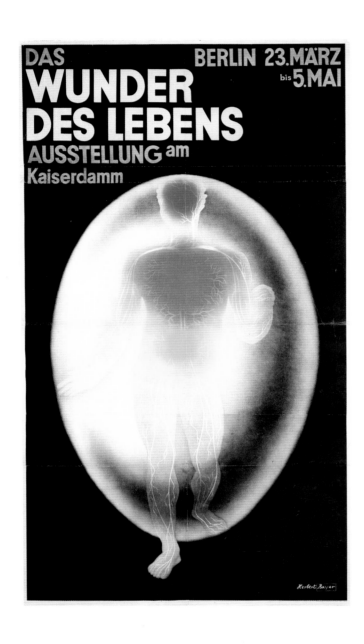

HERBERT BAYER

200 Das Wunder des Lebens
The Miracle of Life
1934
Lithograph
58 × 32⅝"
Given anonymously
· · · · · · · · · · · · ·
Exhibition poster

HANS ERNI

201 Atomkrieg Nein
Atomic War No
1954
Offset lithograph
50 × 35"
Gift of the designer

RUODI BARTH AND
FRITZ BÜHLER

202 Nivea
1948
Lithograph
50⅛ × 35⅜″
Don Page Fund
·············
Advertisement for skin cream

B. WESTRELL

203 Vademecum
c. 1953
Lithograph
27½ × 19½″
Gift of The Lauder Foundation,
Leonard and Evelyn Lauder Fund
·············
Advertisement for toothpaste

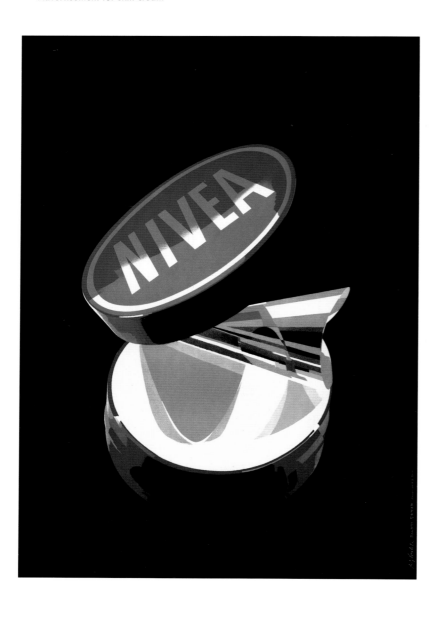

CHARLES KUHN

204 Labyrinthe
  1944
  Lithograph
  50¼ × 35½″
  Given anonymously
  . . . .
  Poster for a monthly publication

FRITZ BÜHLER

205 Film

1945

Offset lithograph

50 × 35½″

**Gift of The Lauder Foundation,
Leonard and Evelyn Lauder Fund**

. . . .

**Poster for international film
festival and congress, Basel**

HERBERT BAYER

206 Olivetti

1953

Offset lithograph

27½ × 19⅝″

Gift of the designer

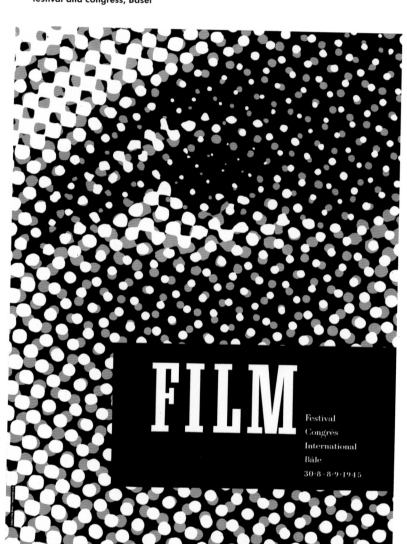

GIOVANNI PINTORI

207 Olivetti
1947
Offset lithograph
37½ × 26¼"
Gift of the designer

HERBERT MATTER

208 K[noll] Single Pedestal Furniture
Designed by Eero Saarinen
c. 1957
Offset lithograph
45 × 26"
Gift of the designer

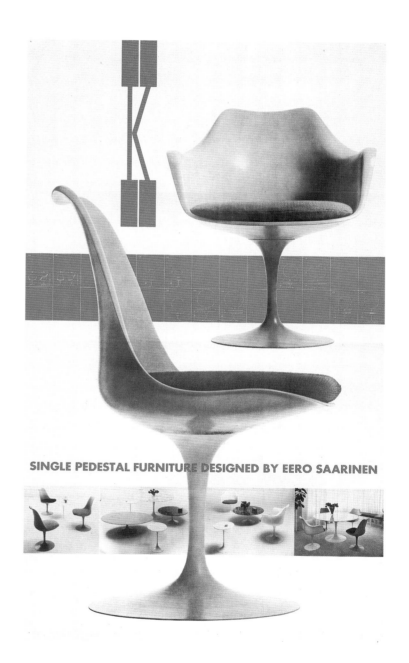

ERIK NITSCHE

209 **Exploring the Universe, General Dynamics**
1958
Lithograph
50 × 35¼"
Gift of General Dynamics Corporation

IVAN CHERMAYEFF

210 **The Mead Library of Ideas 23rd International Annual Report Competition**
c. 1975
Offset lithograph
22 × 17"
Chermayeff and Geismar Fund

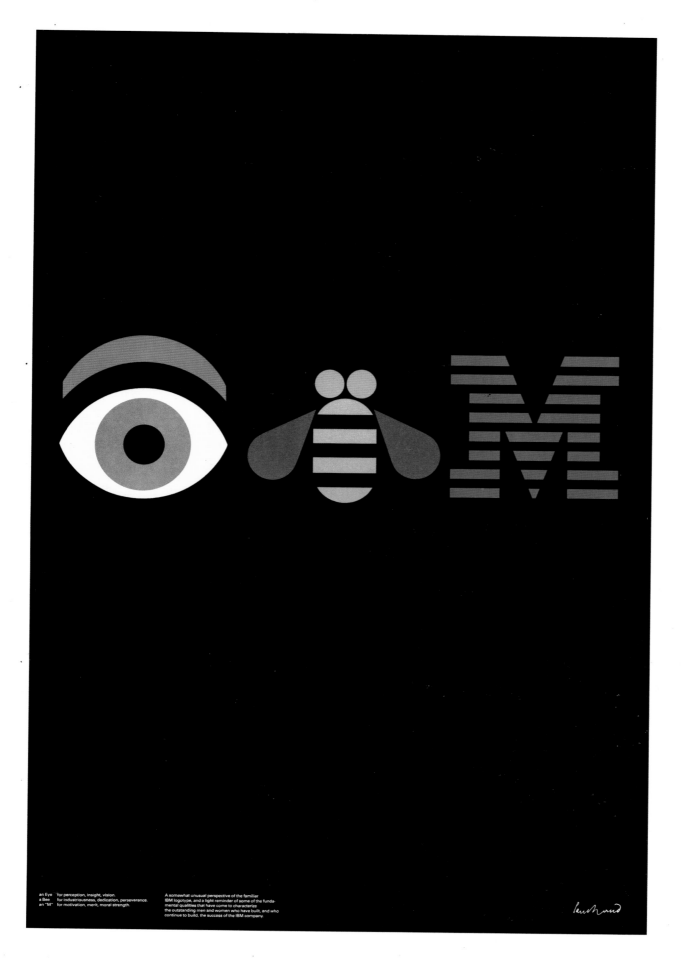

an Eye   for perception, insight, vision.
a Bee   for industriousness, dedication, perseverance.
an "M"   for motivation, merit, moral strength.

A somewhat unusual perspective of the familiar
IBM logotype, and a light reminder of some of the fundamental qualities that have come to characterize
the outstanding men and women who have built, and who
continue to build, the success of the IBM company.

PAUL RAND
211 IBM
1982
Offset lithograph
36 × 24″
Gift of the designer

MAX HUBER

212 7 CIAM
1949
Offset lithograph
18⅝ × 26⅛″
Gift of the designer
....
Poster for seventh international
congress of modern architecture

BRUNO MUNARI

213 Pirelli
1953
Offset lithograph
38 × 26¾″
Gift of the designer
....
Sequence of three posters

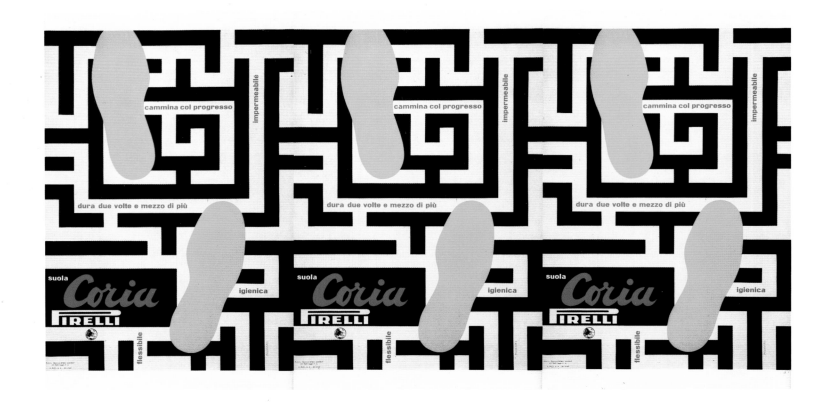

BRUNO MUNARI

214 Campari

1965

Offset lithograph

6′5¼″ × 9′1¼″

Gift of the designer

·············

Advertisement for an aperitif

GIOVANNI PINTORI

215 Olivetti
1950
Offset lithograph
37⅜ × 26¼"
Gift of the designer

WINFRED GAUL

216 Images Meditatives
Meditative Images
1960
Silkscreen
27⅝ × 19⅞"
Gift of the designer
....
Exhibition poster

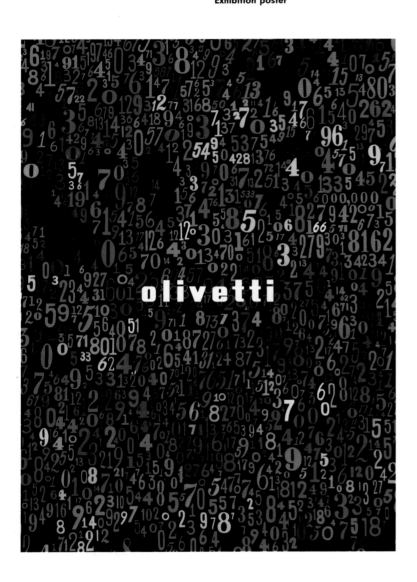

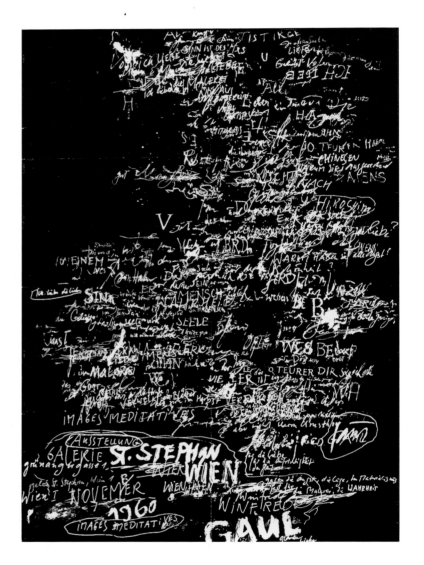

RYUICHI YAMASHIRO

217 Forest Wood
1954
Silkscreen
41 × 29½"
Gift of the designer
....
Poster for forest-
conservation movement

IKKO TANAKA

218 Kanze Noh Play
1961
Silkscreen
41¾ × 28¾"
Gift of the designer
....
Theater poster

第八回産経観世能

第一部十時始
一角仙人　観世静夫
実盛　観世銕之丞

第二部四時始

花筐　梅若泰之
草子洗小町　観世元昭
安宅　観世喜之
土蜘蛛　梅若猶義
梅若万三郎
梅若六郎

舞囃子　唐船　橋岡久太郎

昭和三十六年二月二十六日（日）
大阪産経会館特設能舞台
主催　産経新聞社　大阪新聞社

SIGMAR POLKE

219 **Polke Neue Bilder**
Polke, New Paintings
1967
Offset lithograph
33 × 23¼"
Given anonymously
············
Exhibition poster

ROBERT GRETCZKO AND
CHARLES ZIMMERMAN

220 **"Our Town 1970"**
1964
Offset lithograph
27⅞ × 18"
Gift of Municipal Arts Society
············
Exhibition poster

Sigmar Polke: Neue Bilder. Galerie Heiner Friedrich, München, Maximilianstr 15. Dienstag bis Samstag 10 bis 19 Uhr. 4.–23. April 1967

Exhibition: An exhibit showing proposed urban designs for New York City

Sponsored by the Municipal Art Society, Union Carbide Building 270 Park Ave. N.Y.C. April 6 - May 11

"Our Town 1970"

soweix
schreix
schreib
schreib

la poétique   zur eröffnung
sémantique   am 10. juli
                20 uhr spricht
bilder   william e. simmat
objekte
graphik   galerie gunar
                düsseldorf
10. juli bis   schützenstraße 63
15. august 1965 an der kölner str.

Siebdruck Dr. Simmat Wiesbaden

typographie wolfgang schmidt
(unter verwendung des kodex der
grundgesten aus dem semantischen
manifest von lattanzi + schreib 1961)

MASSIMO VIGNELLI

222 XXXII Biennale Internazionale d'Arte Venezia
1964
Offset lithograph
38 × 27³⁄₁₆″
Gift of the designer
. . . .
Exhibition poster

EMILIO AMBASZ

223 Geigy Graphics
1967
Offset lithograph, diecut
15½ × 15″
Gift of the designer
. . . .
Exhibition poster

FONTANA GALLERIA LA POLENA GENOVA 1-28 OTTOBRE 1966

design: a g fronzoni stampa: officina Lucini Milano

MAX BILL

225 Pevsner, Vantongerloo, Bill
1949
Lithograph
39¼ × 27½″
Gift of the Swiss government
....
Exhibition poster

TAKASHI KONO

226 Ideal Relationship
1955
Silkscreen
28⅝ × 20¼″
Gift of the designer
....
Poster for tea-
ceremony publication

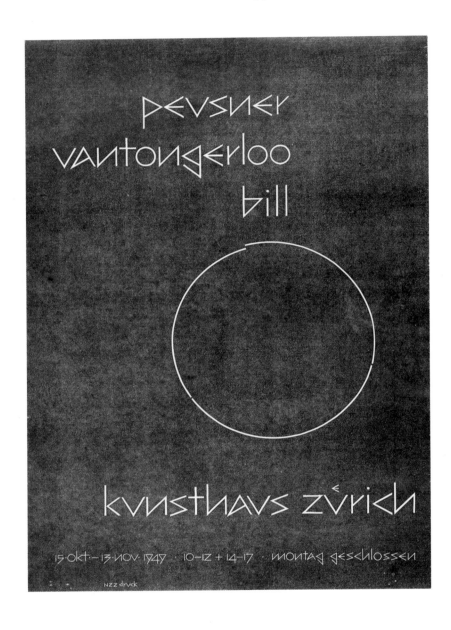

JOSEF MÜLLER-BROCKMANN

227 Musica Viva

1958

Linocut and letterpress

50⅜ × 35⅝″

Gift of the designer

. . . .

Concert poster

ARMIN HOFMANN

228 Robert Jacobsen, Serge Poliakoff

1958

Linocut

50⅜ × 35⁹⁄₁₆″

Gift of the designer

. . . .

Exhibition poster

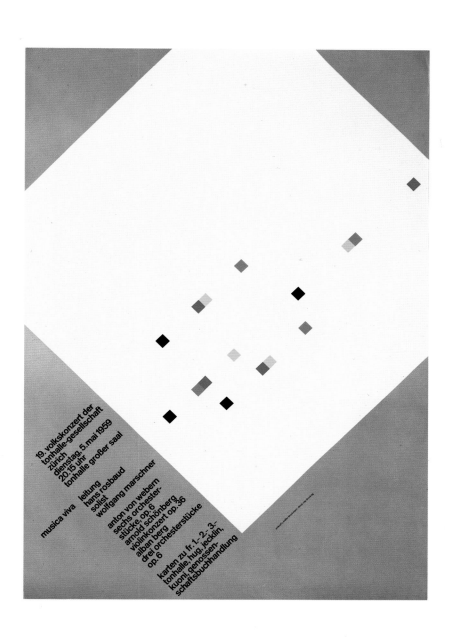

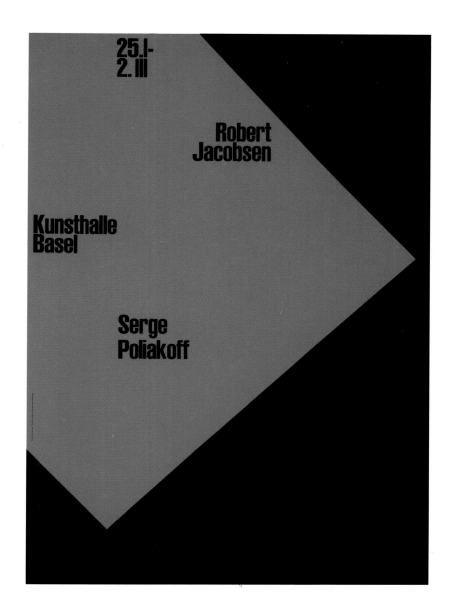

ARMIN HOFMANN

229 Wilhelm Tell
1963
Offset lithograph
50³⁄₁₆ × 35½″
Gift of the designer
· · · · · · · · · · · · ·
Theater poster

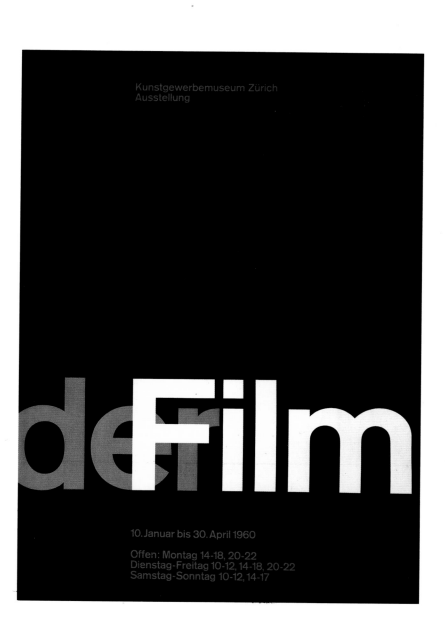

JOSEF MÜLLER-BROCKMANN

232 Weniger Lärm
Less Noise
1960
Offset lithograph
50¼ × 35½"
Acquired by exchange

auch Du bist liberal

KARL GERSTNER
233 Auch Du bist liberal
You too Are Liberal
1959
Offset lithograph
50¼ × 35¼"
Gift of the designer
. . . .
Political poster

FRIEDER AND RENATA GRINDLER

235 Kaspar
1966
Offset lithograph
30 × 20″
Gift of the designers
. . . .
Theater poster

C. H. JOHANSEN

236 Visions
1967
Offset lithograph
35 × 23″
Gift of Joseph H. Heil

MILTON GLASER

237 Dylan
1966
Offset lithograph
33 × 22″
Gift of the designer

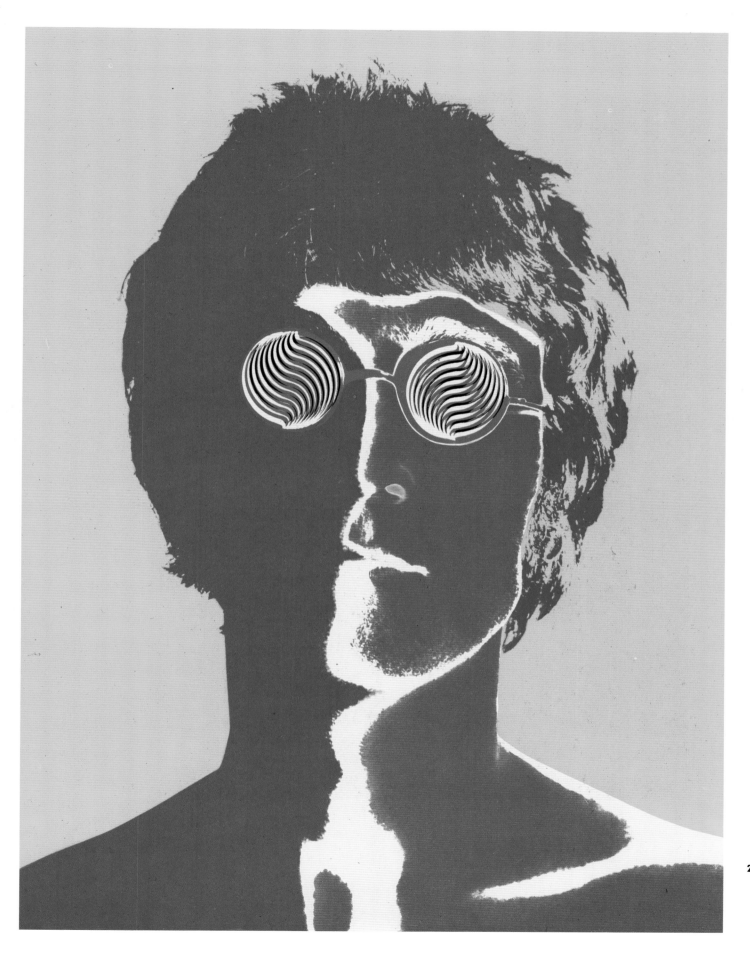

RICHARD AVEDON

238 John Lennon
1967
Offset lithograph
31 × 22½"
Gift of the designer

BIG BROTHER & THE HOLDING CO. • LEE MICHAELS • OXFORD CIRCLE

DANCE·CONCERT
DEC 9-10
FRI SAT
SUTTER AT VANNESS · SAN FRANCISCO 9 P.M.

LIGHTS
BEN VAN METER
ROGER HILLYARD

AVALON BALLROOM

© 1966 FAMILY DOG PROD.

TICKET OUTLETS:
SAN FRANCISCO: The Psychedelic Shop, City Lights Books, Bally Lo, Cedar Alley Coffee House, Sandal Maker (North Beach), Hut T-1 State College
SAUSALITO: Tides Book Shop   *BERKELEY:* Moe's Books, Discount Records   *MENLO PARK:* Kepler's Book Store

The Bindweed Press, San Francisco

VICTOR MOSCOSO

239 Big Brother & the Holding Co.
1966
Offset lithograph
20⅛ × 14"
Gift of the designer
. . . .
Oxford Circle, Big Brother &
the Holding Co., Lee Michaels
Concert poster

ROBERT WESLEY WILSON

240 The Association
1966
Offset lithograph
19¹¹⁄₁₆ × 13¾"
Purchase fund
. . . .
The Association, Along Comes
Mary, Quicksilver Messenger
Service
Concert poster

LEE CONKLIN

241 Procol Harum
1969
Offset lithograph
21¼ × 14⅛"
Gift of the designer
. . . .
Procol Harum, Santana
Concert poster

VICTOR MOSCOSO

242 Junior Wells and His Chicago
Blues Band
1966
Offset lithograph
19⅞ × 14"
Gift of the designer
....
Concert poster

VICTOR MOSCOSO

243 Youngbloods
   1967
   Offset lithograph
   20¼ × 14"
   Peter Stone Poster Fund
   ....
   Youngbloods, The Other
   Half, Mad River
   Concert poster

VICTOR MOSCOSO

244 Hawaii Pop Rock Festival
   1967
   Offset lithograph
   20¼ × 14"
   Gift of the designer
   ··············
   The Canned Heat, Country
   Joe & the Fish, Luke's
   Pineapple Store, Blues
   Crew, Tony Sonoda

VICTOR MOSCOSO

245 Otis Rush
   1967
   Offset lithograph
   20 × 14"
   Gift of the designer
   ··············
   Concert poster

BOB SCHNEPF

246 Avalon Ballroom
   1967
   Offset lithograph
   28 × 10⅞"
   Given anonymously
   ··············
   Jim Kweskin & His Jug Band,
   Country Joe & the Fish,
   Lee Michaels, Blue Cheer
   Concert poster

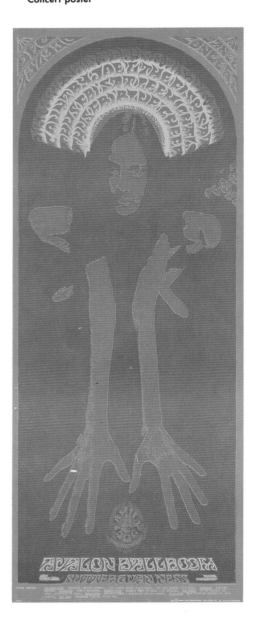

VICTOR MOSCOSO

247 Quicksilver Messenger Service
1967
Offset lithograph
20¼ × 14"
Gift of the designer
. . . .
Quicksilver Messenger Service, Big
Brother & the Holding Company,
Blue Cheer
Concert poster

PETER MAX

248 #12 Captain Midnight
1966
Offset lithograph
36 × 24"
Gift of East Hampton Gallery,
New York

JOHANNES REYN

249 IBM, Rev-up
1967
Silkscreen
34¾ × 24¾"
Gift of Roberts and Reyn, Inc.

OFFICE PRODUCTS DIVISION

REV-UP

great architecture in chicago

TOMOKO MIHO

**250 Great Architecture in Chicago
1967
Silkscreen on metallic paper
50 × 35″
Gift of Container Corporation
of America**

EDUARDO PAOLOZZI

251 Universal Electronic Vacuum
1967
Silkscreen
34 × 24³⁄₁₆″
Gift of Pace Gallery
. . . .
Exhibition poster

WIM CROUWEL

252 Vorm Gevers
Form Givers
1968
Offset lithograph
37³⁄₁₆ × 24¹⁵⁄₁₆″
Gift of the designer
. . . .
Exhibition poster

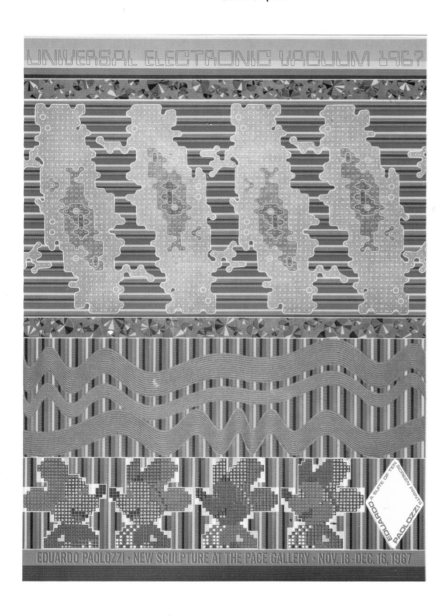

Juan Carlos Distéfano, Rubén
Fontana, and Carlos Soler

253 Olivetti: Diseño y Productos
Olivetti: Designs and Products
1969
Offset lithograph
28½ × 42½″
Gift of the designers
. . . .
Exhibition poster

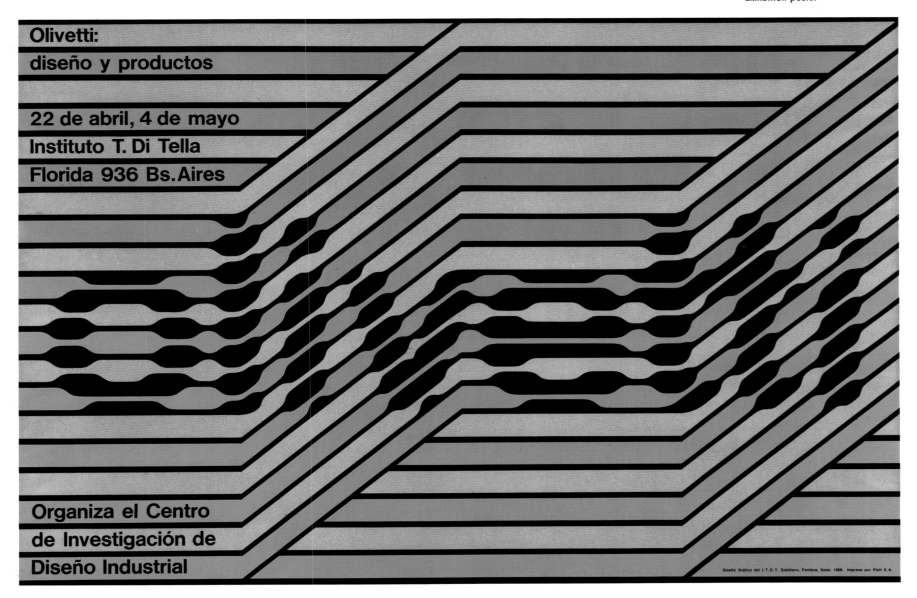

ANDY WARHOL

254 Campbell's Tomato Soup
1966
Silkscreen
24 × 17"
Given anonymously
. . . .
Exhibition poster in
form of shopping bag

ANDY WARHOL

255 Fifth New York Film
Festival—Lincoln Center
1967
Silkscreen
45 × 24"
Peter Stone Poster Fund

Bank by Andy Warhol. Gaudy savings by RCA Color Scanner. Pretty as a pigture, huh?

ANDY WARHOL

256 Bank by Andy Warhol
1968
Offset lithograph
29⅞ × 45¼″
Poster fund
. . . .
**Advertisement for
printing equipment**

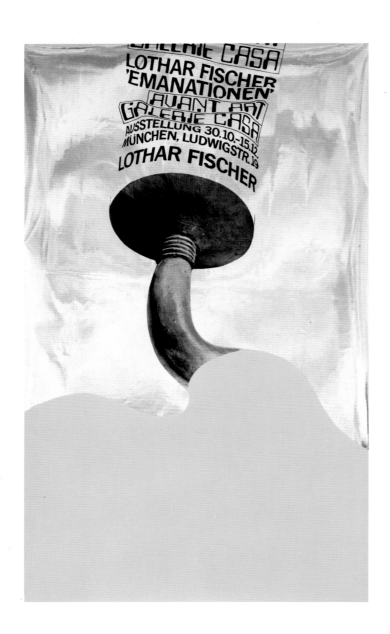

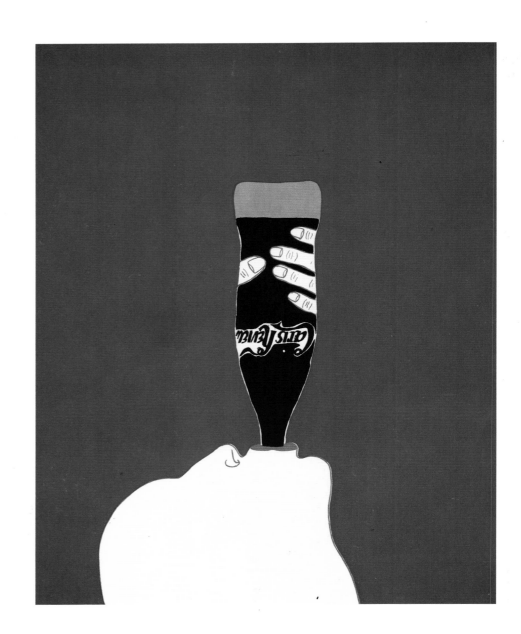

LOTHAR FISCHER

257 Lothar Fischer "Emanationen"
Lothar Fischer "Emanations"
1968
Silkscreen on mylar
37¼ × 22"
Gift of Galerie Casa, Munich
· · · · · · · · · · · ·
Exhibition poster

MARISOL

258 Paris Review
1967
Silkscreen
32½ × 26"
Gift of Page, Arbitrio & Resen
· · · · · · · · · · · ·
Poster for a magazine

ROBERT ABEL

259 7 Up
1975
Offset lithograph
45½ × 59½″
Gift of Leslie Schreyer
. . . .
Advertisement for a beverage

MICHAEL ENGLISH

260 Love Festival
1967
Silkscreen
29⅞ × 40″
Gift of P. Reyner Banham

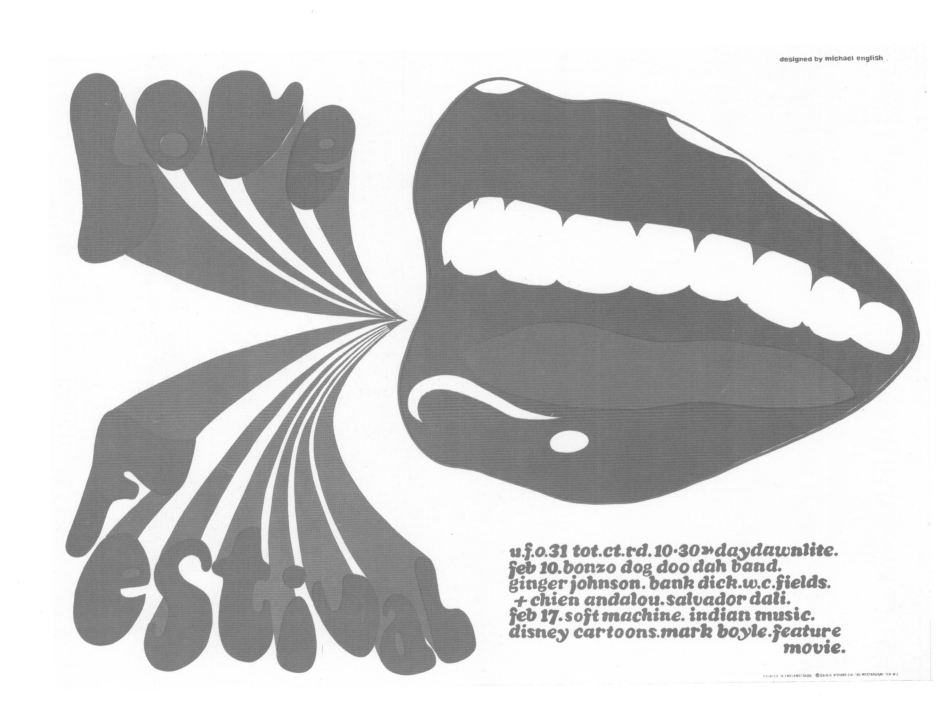

261 Kamienne Niebo
Stone Sky
1979
Offset lithograph
51¼ × 38⅛"
Gift of the designer
. . . .
Theater poster

262 Dakönnen Sie Giftdraufnehmen!
You Bet Your Life!
1984
Offset lithograph
46¾ × 33"
Gift of the designer
. . . .
Political cabaret poster

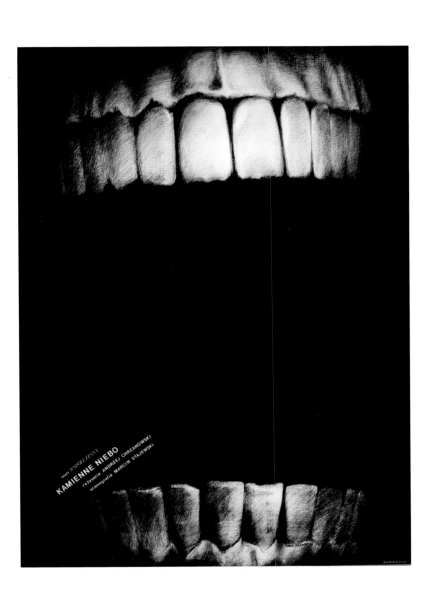

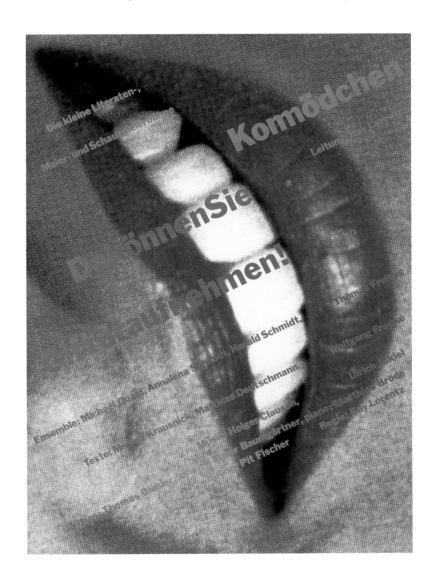

ELENA SERRANO

263 Day of the Heroic Guerrilla
  1968
  Offset lithograph
  19½ × 13⅛″
  Gift of OSPAAAL
  ··············
  Political poster

DENNIS WHEELER

264 Life
  1963
  Offset lithograph
  46¾ × 59½″
  Gift of Time, Inc.
  ··············
  Poster for the magazine

End Bad Breath.

SEYMOUR CHWAST

265 End Bad Breath.
1967
Offset lithograph
37 × 24"
Gift of Pushpin Studios
. . . .
Antiwar poster

CRISTOS GIANAKOS

266 Send Our Boys Home
1966
Offset lithograph
12¼ × 17"
Gift of the designer
. . . .
Antiwar poster

SEND OUR BOYS HOME

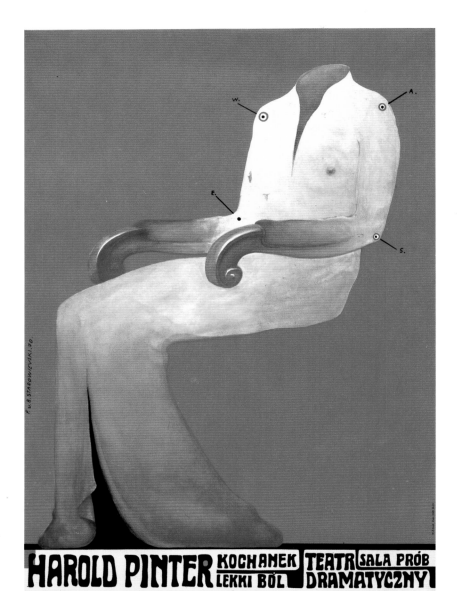

FRANCISZEK STAROWIEYSKI

267 Harold Pinter, Kochanek Lekki Ból
Harold Pinter, The Loved One
1970
Offset lithograph
32⅝ × 22¹⁵⁄₁₆"
Gift of the designer
. . . .
Theater poster

ROMAN CIEŚLEWICZ

268 Strawinski Persefona
1961
Offset lithograph
38 × 26⅝"
Gift of the designer
. . . .
Opera poster

KAFKA

PROCES

ROMAN CIEŚLEWICZ

269 Kafka Proces
Kafka, Trial
1964
Offset lithograph
32¼ × 21½"
Gift of the designer
....
Theater poster

MACIEJ URBANIEC
270 Cyrk
Circus
1970
Offset lithograph
38½ × 26"
Given anonymously

JAN LENICA

271 Polske Surrealister
Polish Surrealists
1970
Offset lithograph
38¼ × 26⅝"
Gift of the designer
. . . .
Exhibition poster

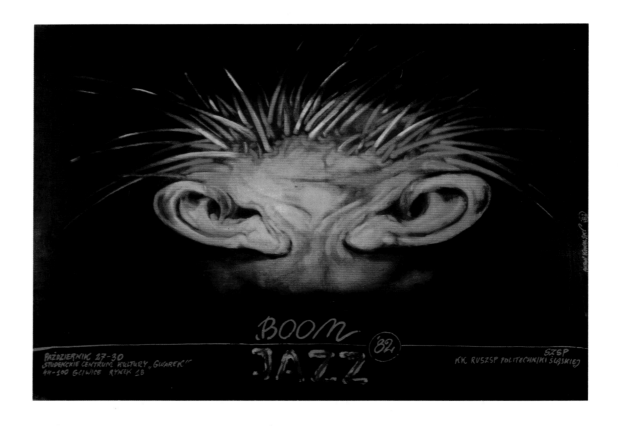

ANTONI KOWALSKI

272 Boom, Jazz '82
1984
Offset lithograph
26½ × 37⅝"
Gift of the designer
. . . .
Concert poster

MIECZYSLAW GÓROWSKI

273 Mieczyslaw Górowski Plakaty
Mieczyslaw Górowski Posters
1984
Offset lithograph
32⅝ × 23¼"
Gift of the designer
. . . .
Exhibition poster

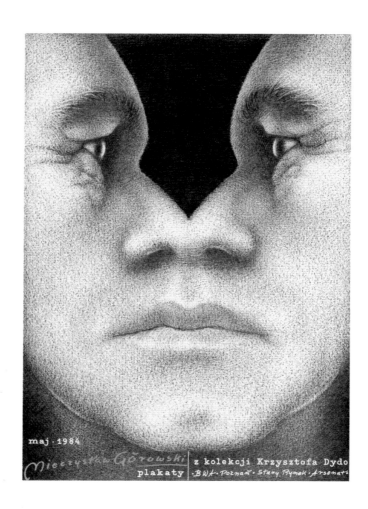

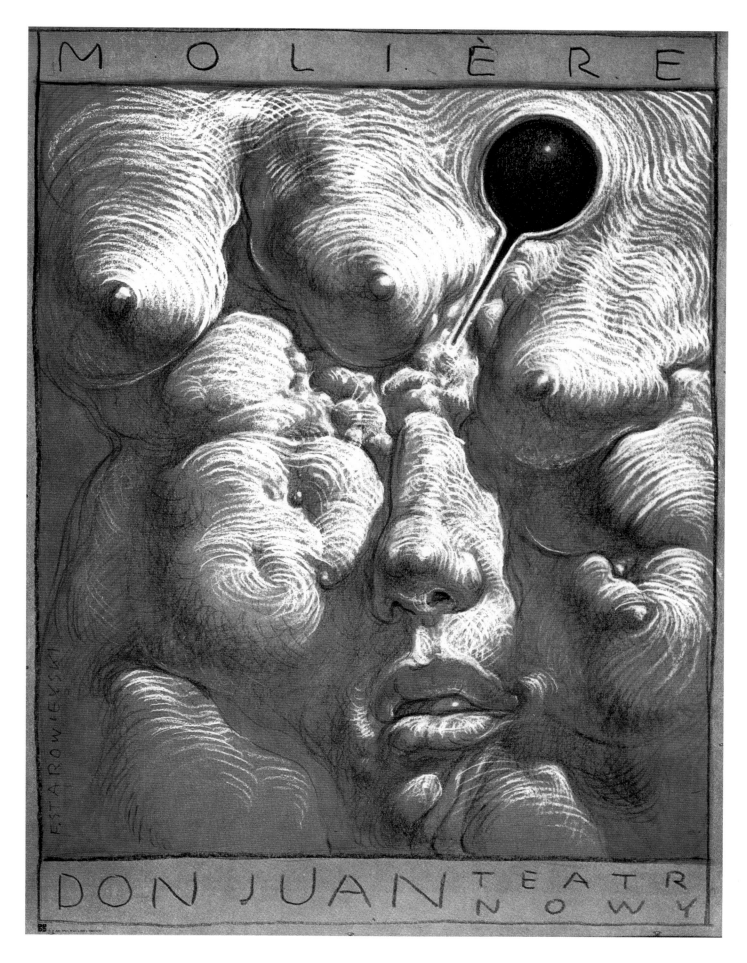

FRANCISZEK STAROWIEYSKI

274 Molière, Don Juan
  1983
  Offset lithograph
  35½ × 26½″
  Gift of the designer
  ··············
  Theater poster

TADANORI YOKOO

275 Made in Japan, Tadanori Yokoo
1965
Silkscreen
43 × 31⅛"
Gift of the designer
....
Exhibition poster

TADANORI YOKOO

276 The City and Design
1966
Silkscreen
41 × 29½"
Gift of the designer
....
Poster for a book by Isamu Kurita

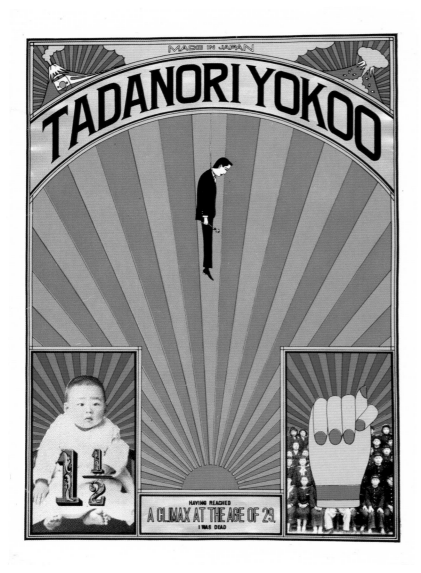

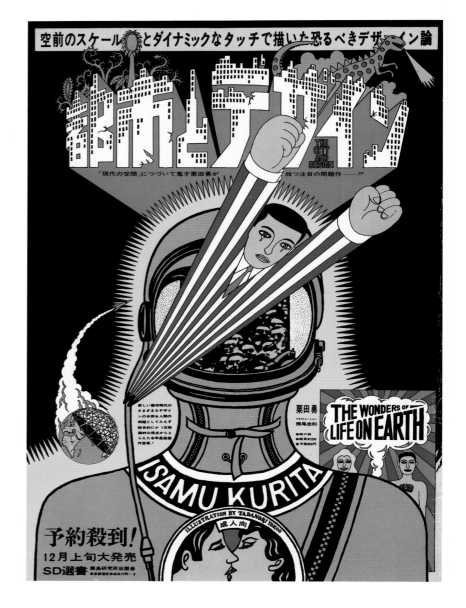

TADANORI YOKOO

277 Ballad to an Amputated
Little Finger
1967
Silkscreen
40½ × 28½"
Gift of the designer
. . . .
Poster for a book

Tadanori Yokoo

278 National Bunraku Theater
1971
Silkscreen
40 × 28½"
Gift of the designer
....
Puppet theater poster

237

IKKO TANAKA

KOICHI SATO

280 **Nihon Buyo**
1981
Offset lithograph
40½ × 28¾"
Gift of College of Fine Arts, UCLA
· · · · · · · · · · · · · ·
Poster for a dance performance

281 **New Music Media**
New Magic Media
1974
Silkscreen
40½ × 28¾"
Gift of the designer
· · · · · · · · · · · · · ·
Concert poster

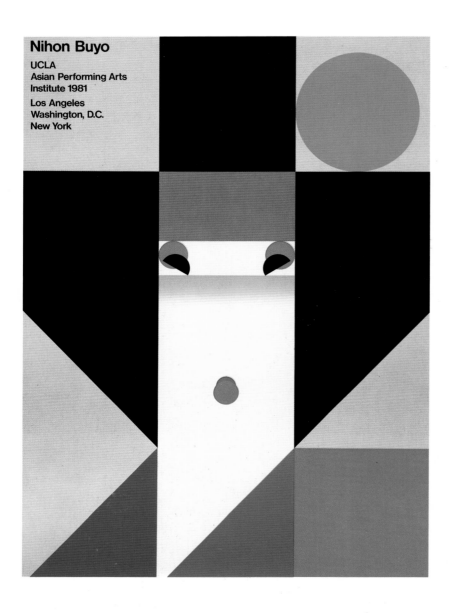

TAKENOBU IGARASHI

282 Zen
  1981
  Offset lithograph
  28⁹⁄₁₆ × 40⁷⁄₁₆″
  Gift of Leonard A. Lauder
  ....
  Advertisement for a design firm

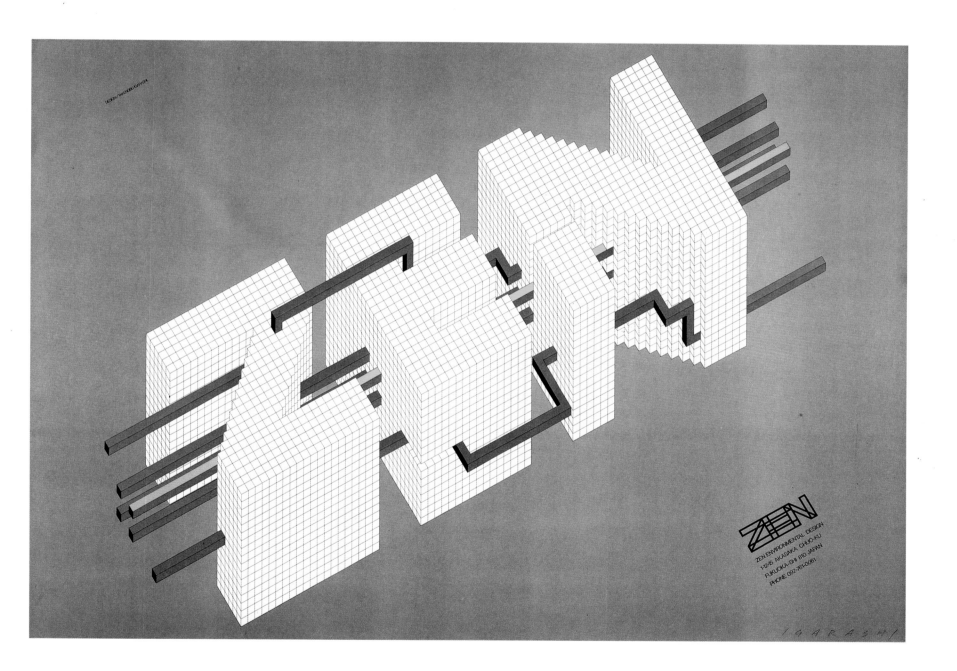

MASATOSHI TODA

**283 Parco, A Woman's Skin
Absorbs Dreams**
1983
Silkscreen
43 × 31"
Gift of the designer
. . . .
**Advertisement for a
department store**

TAKAO SASAI

284 Handle Me
1986
Offset lithograph
33 × 23⅜"
**Gift of the designer, Works Inc.,
and Rockwell Art Center**
. . . .
Poster for a beauty (hand) contest

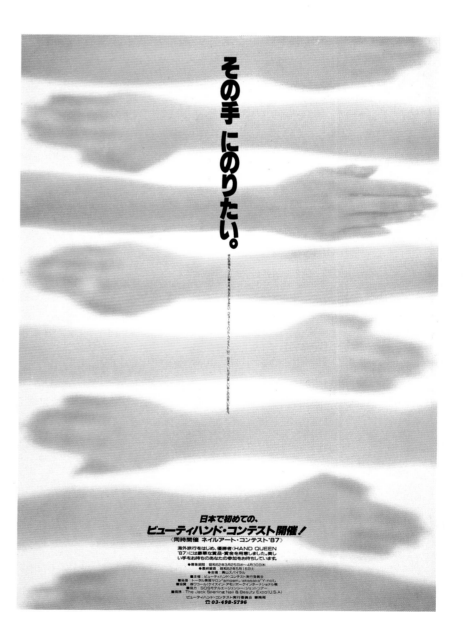

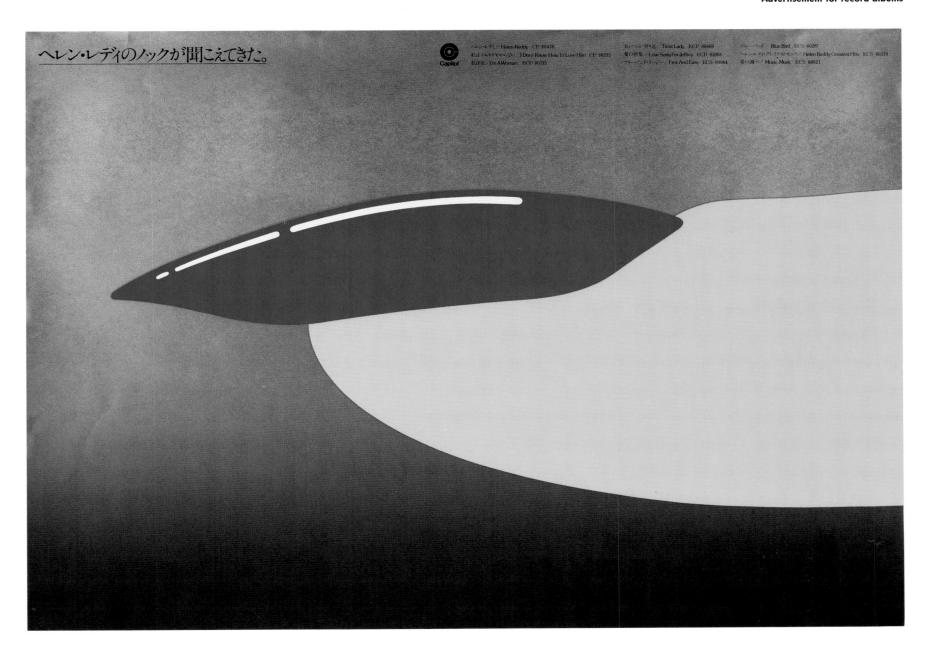

241

287 Punktum.
Point.
1982
Offset lithograph
33¹⁄₁₆ × 46⁷⁄₈″
Gift of the designer
. . . .
Advertisement for a printing
company

Punktum.

Kirschbaum Laserscan Düsseldorf   Offsetdruck Team Dortmund

**Deutschland
1930-1939
Verbot Anpassung Exil**

Im Rahmen der Ausstellung
finden im grossen Vortragssaal
des Kunsthauses
täglich Filmvorführungen statt:

12. August - 2. Oktober

kunsthaus zürich

Dienstag und Mittwoch 18.15 Uhr
Donnerstag 15.00 Uhr und 18.15 Uhr
Freitag 18.15 Uhr
Samstag 15.00 Uhr
Sonntag 10.30 Uhr und 15.00 Uhr

Öffnungszeiten:
Dienstag bis Freitag 10-21 Uhr
Samstag und Sonntag 10-17 Uhr
Montag 14-17 Uhr
Bettag, 18. September, geschlossen

Gestaltung: Hofstetter + Wägli, Zürich
Druck: Lichtdruck AG, Dielsdorf Litho: Offset-Repro AG

CHRISTOFF MARTIN HOFSTETTER

**288 Deutschland 1930–1939, Verbot
Anpassung Exil**

*Germany 1930–1939, Suppression,
Assimilation, Exile*

1977

Offset lithograph

50 × 35³⁄₁₆″

Gift of the designer

. . . .

Exhibition poster

HELMUT SCHMIDT-RHEN

289 Kunst nach Wirklichkeit, Ein neuer Realismus in Amerika und in Europa
Art after Reality, A New Realism in America and Europe
1978
Offset lithograph
23⅜ × 33″
Gift of the designer
....
Exhibition poster

Yusaku Kamekura

290 Hiroshima Appeals
1983
Offset lithograph
40½ × 28⅝"
Given anonymously

Gunter Rambow

291 Utopie Dynamit
1976
Offset lithograph
46½ × 32¾"
Gift of the designer
. . . .
Poster for a literary publication

Jukka Veistola

292 UNICEF
1969
Offset lithograph
39½ × 27½"
Gift of the designer

Tapio Salmelainen and
Jukka Veistola

293 DDT
1970
Offset lithograph
47¼ × 31½"
Gift of the designers

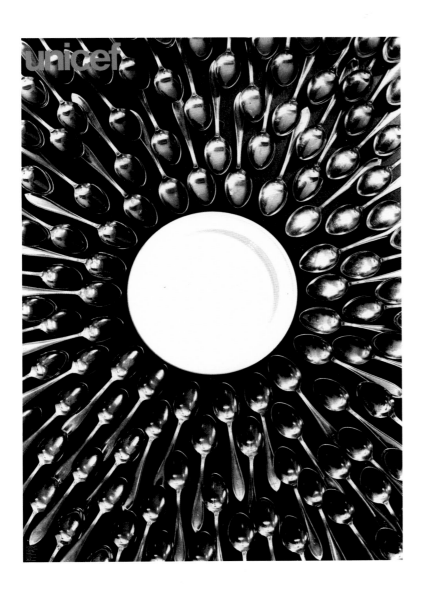

NIKLAUS TROXLER

294 McCoy Tyner Sextet
1980
Offset lithograph
50⅜ × 35⅝"
Gift of The Lauder Foundation,
Leonard and Evelyn Lauder Fund
. . . .
Concert poster

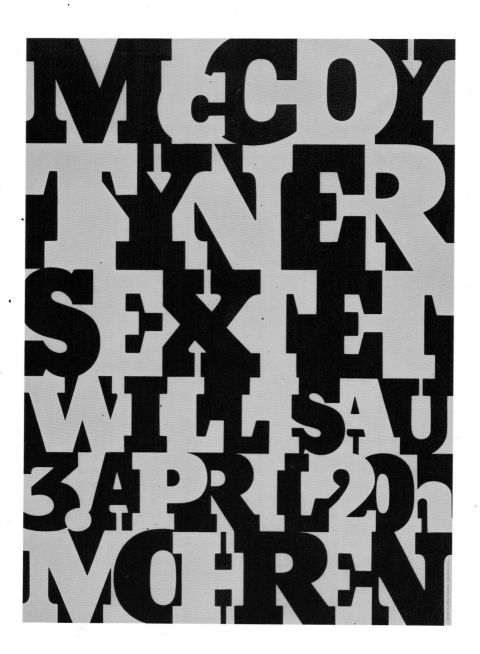

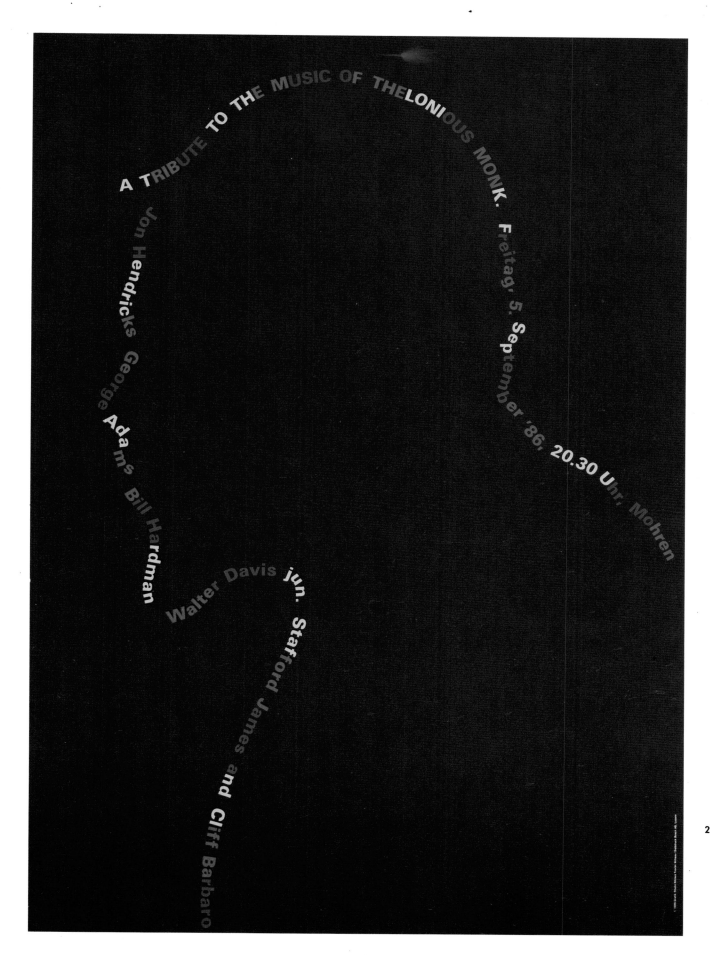

296 Das Schweizer Plakat
The Swiss Poster
1984
Offset lithograph
47¼ × 33⅛″
Gift of the designer
....
Exhibition poster

KOICHI SATO

297 **Morisawa & Company, Ltd.**
1983
Silkscreen
40½ × 28⅝"
Gift of the designer
. . . .
Advertisement for a printing company

APRIL GREIMAN

298 **Snow White + the Seven Pixels**
1986
Offset lithograph
36 × 24"
Gift of the designer
. . . .
Poster for a lecture

ANDRZEJ PAGOWSKI

299 Uśmiech Wilka
Wolf's Smile
1982
Offset lithograph
26⅜ × 37"
Purchase fund
. . . .
Theater poster

SEITARO KURODA

300 Seibu
1981
Silkscreen
40½ × 28½"
Gift of the designer
. . . .
**Poster for an exhibition at
a department store**

GRAPUS

301 On Y Va
Let's Go
1977
Offset lithograph
47¼ × 37½"
Gift of the designer
. . . .
*Everybody to Ivry, to the Party,
Toward Change!*
Political poster

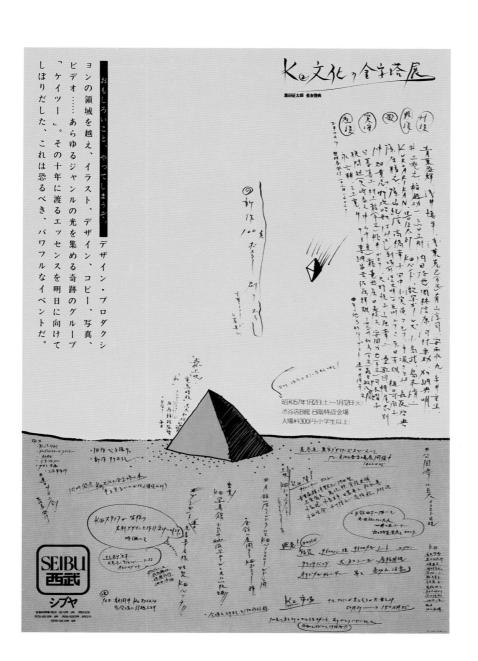

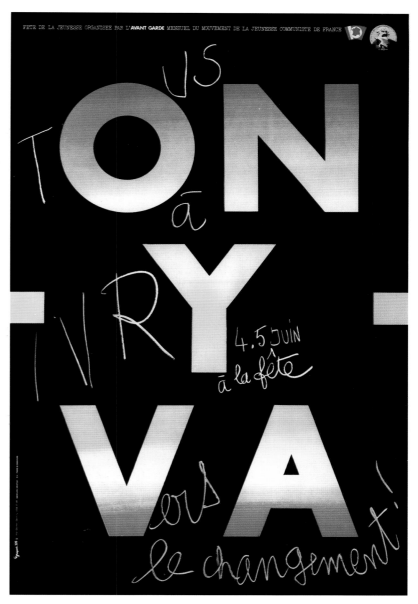

253

BIBLIOGRAPHY

The bibliographic documentation below is arranged in four sections. The first three contain an international selection of books and exhibition catalogues under the following headings: General Works, Books by Country, and Individual Designers. The first section consists of surveys and works including posters of more than one country. The second and third divisions are limited to countries and designers represented in this publication. The fourth section, Periodicals, provides a brief listing of journals devoted solely to the poster.

GENERAL WORKS

Alexandre, Arsène; Spielmann, M. H.; Bunner, H. C.; and Jaccaci, August (eds.). *The Modern Poster*. New York: Charles Scribner's Sons, 1895. 117 pp.

Allner, Walter. *Posters*. New York: Reinhold Publishing Corporation, 1952. 119 pp.

Bauwens, M.; Hayashi, T.; Laforgue, J.; Meier-Graefe, J.; and Pennell, J. *Les affiches étrangères illustrées*. Paris: Boudet, 1897. 206 pp.

Behne, Adolf; Landau, P.; and Löwing, H. *Das politische Plakat*. Berlin: Verlag "Das Plakat," 1919. 49 pp. 22 plates.

Bock, Henning, and Heusinger, Christian (eds.). *Europäischer Jugendstil. Druckgraphik, Handzeichnungen und Aquarelle, Plakate, Illustrationen und Buchkunst um 1900*. Bremen: Kunsthalle, 1965. 227 pp. (Exhibition catalogue.)

Bolton, Charles Knowles. *A Descriptive Catalogue of Posters, Chiefly American, in the Collection of Charles Knowles Bolton with Biographical Notes and Bibliography, May MDCCCXCV*. Boston: Winthrop B. Jones, 1895. 16 pp.

————. *The Reign of the Poster*. Boston: Winthrop B. Jones, 1895.

Brinton, Christian; Cassandre, A. M.; and Coiner, Charles. *New Poster*. Philadelphia: Franklin Institute of the State of Pennsylvania, 1937. 64 pp. (Exhibition catalogue.)

Constantine, Mildred (ed.). *The Poster Collection: Recent Acquisitions*. New York: The Museum of Modern Art, 1951. 5 pp. (Published as *The Museum of Modern Art Bulletin*, vol. 18, no. 4 [June 1951].)

————. *Word and Image: Posters from the Collection of The Museum of Modern Art*. Essay by Alan M. Fern. New York: The Museum of Modern Art, 1968. 160 pp. (Exhibition catalogue.)

Crawford, Anthony R. (ed.). *Posters of World War I and World War II in the George C. Marshall Research Foundation*. Introduction by O. W. Riegel. Charlottesville, Va.: The University Press of Virginia, 1979. 128 pp.

Diederich, Reiner, and Grübling, Richard (eds.). *"Wir haben die Erde nur geborgt." Plakate gegen Umweltzerstörung*. Weinhem and Basel: Beltz Verlag, 1986. 124 pp.

Diederich, Reiner; Grübling, Richard; and Trapp, Horst (eds.). *Plakate gegen den Krieg*. Weinhem and Basel: Beltz Verlag, 1983. 96 pp.

Edwards, Gregory J. *International Film Poster Book: The Role of the Poster in Cinema Art, Advertising and History*. Topsfield, Mass.: Salem House Ltd., 1985. 224 pp.

Friedman, Mildred (ed.). *The 20th Century Poster: Design of the Avant-Garde*. Essays by Dawn Ades, Robert Brown, Alma Law, Armin Hofmann, and Merrill C. Berman. New York: Abbeville Press, 1984. 216 pp. (Exhibition catalogue.)

Das frühe Plakat in Europa und den USA. 4 vols. Berlin: Gebr. Mann Verlag, 1973–80. Vol. 1: *Grossbritannien, Vereinigte Staaten von Nordamerika* (1973). Edited by Ruth Malhotra and Christina Thon. 227 pp. Vol. 2: *Frankreich und Belgien* (1977). Edited by Ruth Malhotra, Marjan Rinkleff, and Bernd Schälicke. 423 pp. Vols. 3 and 4: *Deutschland* (1980). Edited by Helga Hollmann, Ruth Malhotra, Alexander Pilipczuk, Helga Prignitz, and Christina Thon. Vol. 3: 506 pp.; vol. 4: 363 plates.

Grautoff, Otto. *Das moderne Plakat am Ende des 19.Jahrhunderts*. Leipzig, 1899.

Grushkin, Paul D. *The Rock Poster*. New York: Abbeville Press, 1987. 432 pp.

de Harak, Rudolph (ed.). *Posters by Members of the Alliance Graphique Internationale 1960–1985*. New York: Rizzoli International, 1986. 200 pp.

Hardie, Martin, and Sabin, Arthur K. (eds.). *War Posters Issued by Belligerent and Neutral Nations, 1914–1919*. London: A. F. & C. Black, 1920. 46 pp. 77 plates.

Hiatt, Charles. *Picture Posters*. London: George Bell & Sons, 1895. 367 pp. Reprinted 1976.

Kämpfer, Frank. *"Der rote Keil." Das politische Plakat, Theorie und Geschichte*. Berlin: Gebr. Mann Verlag, 1985. 325 pp.

Kauffer, Edward McKnight. *The Art of the Poster: Its Origin, Evolution, Purpose*. New York: Albert & Charles Boni, 1928. 190 pp.

Levy, Albert. *L'apartheid: Le dos au mur*. Preface by Alain Weill. Paris: Droit et Liberté Editions, Musée de l'Affiche et de la Publicité, 1982. 90 pp. (Exhibition catalogue.)

Maindron, Ernst. *Les affiches illustrées*. Paris: H. Launette, 1886. 160 pp.

————. *Les affiches illustrées, 1886–1895*. Paris: G. Boudet, 1896. 251 pp.

Mellinghoff, Frieder (ed.). *Aufbruch in das mobile Jahrhundert: Verkehrsmittel auf Plakaten*. Dortmund: Harenberg Kommunikation, 1981. 168 pp.

————. *Triennale '83: Die besten Plakate der Jahre 1980–83*. Essen: Deutsches Plakat Museum, 1984. 78 pp. (Exhibition catalogue.)

Miedzynarodoivy Plakat Revolucyjny, 1917–1967. Warsaw: Muzeum Lenina, 1967. 84 pp.

Müller-Brockmann, Josef and Shizuko. *History of the Poster*. Zurich: ABC Verlag, 1971. 244 pp.

Piettre, J. H. *Affiches de presse; almanachs—feuilletons—journaux*. Preface by Henri Amouroux. Paris: Musée-Galerie de la Seita, 1984. 38 pp. (Exhibition catalogue.)

Polumbaum, Nyna Brael (ed.). *Save Life on Earth*. Introduction by Bernard Lown; statements by John Hersey, Yevgeny Yevtushenko, Robert Rozhdestvenski, Ai Qing, Christa Wolf, and Louise Valenzuela. Berlin: Elefanten Press, 1986. 112 pp.

Price, Charles Matlack. *Poster Design*. Rev. ed. New York: G. W. Bricka, 1922. 370 pp.

Ravera, Camilla; Ashton, Dore; and Italiani, Giulio C. *Per la rivoluzione per la patria per la famiglia e per le donne: 100 anni di manifesti politici nel mondo*. Venice: Marsilio Editori, 1978. 119 pp.

Rennert, Jack. *100 Years of Bicycle Posters*. New York: Harper & Row, Darien House, 1973. 112 pp.

Richardson, E. C. *Princeton University Library War Poster Collections*. Princeton: Princeton University Library, 1919. 2 vols. n.p. (These two volumes of reproductions and descriptions were apparently published only in photostat for a limited distribution.)

Rickards, Maurice. *Banned Posters*. Park Ridge, N.J.: Noyes Press, 1972. 72 pp.

Ruben, Paul (ed.). *Die Reklame, ihre Kunst und Wissenschaft*. Berlin: Verlag für Sozialpolitik, 1913. Vol. 1: 360 pp. Berlin: Hermann Paetel Verlag, 1914. Vol. 2: 304 pp.

Sachs, Hans J. *The World's Largest Poster Collection, 1896–1938*. New York, 1957. 44 pp. (An account of Sachs's collections, which were confiscated by the Nazis and are now in the Museum für Deutsche Geschichte [Berlin].)

Sailer, Anton. *Das Plakat*. Munich: Karl Thiemig, 1965. 207 pp.

Samaranch, Juan Antonio. *L'olympisme par l'affiche: 1896–1984. Olympism through Posters*. Lausanne: International Olympic Committee, 1983. 189 pp.

Schardt, Hermann (intro.). *Das politische Plakat der Welt*. Statements by Heinz Kuhn and Dr. Rewoldt; essays by Thomas Trumpp and Carl Hundhausen. Essen: Deutsches Plakat-Museum, 1973. n.p. (Exhibition catalogue; text in German and English.)

Schindler, Herbert. *Monografie des Plakats: Entwicklung, Stil, Design*. Munich: Süddeutscher Verlag, 1972. 275 pp.

Schockel, Erwin. *Das politische Plakat: Eine psychologische Betrachtung*. Munich: Eigentum der NSDAP, Franz Eher Nachf., 1938. 248 pp.

Semenov, E. (ed.). *Osventsim predosteregaet; vystavka plakata*. Texts by T. Svebotska and K. Smolen'. Moscow: Sovetskii khudozhnik, 1986. 32 pp. (Catalogue for an exhibition of Holocaust posters.)

Shackleton, J. T. *Golden Age of the Railway Poster*. London: New English Library; Secaucus, N.J.: Chartwell Books, 1976. 128 pp.

Sheldon, Cyril. *A History of Poster Advertising*. London: Chapman and Hall, 1937. 316 pp.

Spielmann, Heinz. *Plakat und Buchkunst um 1900*. Hamburg: Museum für Kunst und Gewerbe, 1963. 109 pp.

Spielmann, Heinz; Sailer, Anton; and Krause, Ingrid (eds.). *Internationale Plakate 1871–1971*. Munich: Haus der Kunst, 1971. n.p. (Exhibition catalogue.)

Sponsel, Jean Louis. *Das moderne Plakat*. Dresden: Gerhard Kühtmann, 1897. 316 pp.

Stölzl, Christoph (for.). *Zwischen kaltem Krieg und Wirtschaftswunder: Deutsche und europäische Plakate 1945–1959. Eine Ausstellung aus den Beständen der Plakatsammlung des Münchner Stadtmuseums*. Statements by Heinrich Böll, Peter Härtling, and Günter Kunert; essays by Volker Duvigneau, Wilfried Loth, Andreas Ley, and Ulrich Kurowski. Munich: Münchner Stadtmuseum, 1982. 349 pp. (Exhibition catalogue.)

Weill, Alain. *The Poster: A Worldwide Survey and History*. Boston: G. K. Hall, 1985. 424 pp. (Translation of *L'affiche dans le monde* [1984].)

_____. *Les réclames des années 50*. Paris: Le Dernier Terrain Vague, 1983. 95 pp.

Wember, Paul. *Die Jugend der Plakate 1887–1917*. Krefeld: Kaiser Wilhelm Museum, 1961. 342 pp.

Weston, Walter von Zur. *Reklamekunst*. Berlin and Leipzig: Verlag von Velhagen & Klasing, 1914. 164 pp.

_____. *Reklamekunst aus zwei Jahrtausenden*. Berlin: Eigenbröder, 1925. 321 pp.

Wichmann, Hans (ed.). *Warenplakate, Meisterplakate von der Jahrhundertwende bis Heute: Eine Auswahl aus den verborgenen Depots*. Munich: Die Neue Sammlung, 1981. 47 pp. (Exhibition catalogue.)

Whitney, John Hay. *Posters for Defense*. New York: The Museum of Modern Art, 1941. 12 pp. (Published as *The Bulletin of The Museum of Modern Art*, vol. 8, no. 6 [September 1941].)

BOOKS BY COUNTRY

Austria

Koschatzky, Walter, and Kossatz, Horst-Herbert. *Ornamentale Plakatkunst. Wiener Jugendstil 1897–1914*. Salzburg, 1970. 31 pp. 34 plates.

Libesny, Kurt (ed.); Zitter, Josef; and Schürff, Hans. *Das österreichische Plakat*. Vienna: Museum für Kunst und Industrie, 1929. 55 pp.

Mascha, Ottokar. *Österreichische Plakatkunst*. Vienna: J. Löwy, 1915. 8 pp. 124 plates.

Belgium

Beaumont, Alexandre Demeure de. *L'affiche belge*. Toulouse, 1897. 134 pp.

Delavoy, Robert L. (intro.). *Henry van de Velde, 1863–1957*. Essays by Delavoy, R. Verwilghen, L. Lebeer, Fernand Baudin, and Marie Kisselin. Brussels: Palais des Beaux-Arts, 1963. 115 pp. (Exhibition catalogue.)

Hammacher, Abraham M. *Le monde de Henry van de Velde*. Antwerp: Edition Fonds Mercater; Paris: Librairie Hachette, 1967. 353 pp. (Translation of *De Wereld van Henry van de Velde* [1967].)

_____. *Musées Royaux des Beaux-Arts de Belgique. Le groupe de XX et son temps*. Preface by F. C. Legrand. Brussels: Musées Royaux des Beaux-Arts de Belgique, 1962. 148 pp. (Exhibition catalogue.)

Weill, Alain (ed.). *L'affiche en belgique 1880–1980*. Preface by Geneviève Gaëtan-Picon; introduction by Günter Schmiele. Paris: Musée de l'Affiche, 1980. 124 pp. (Exhibition catalogue.)

Cuba

Peterson, Ad (pref.). *Cubaanse affiches*. Compiled by Ada Stroeve. Amsterdam: Stedelijk Museum, 1971. 80 pp. (Exhibition catalogue in English and Dutch.)

Czechoslovakia

Adlerova, Alena. *Plakate aus der Tschechoslowakei*. Munich: Münchner Stadtmuseum, 1965. 18 pp. (Exhibition catalogue.)

Buchmann, Mark; Vlcek, Tomas; and Zuffo, Dario. *CSSR Plakate*. Zurich: Kunstgewerbemuseum, 1973. 28 pp. (Exhibition catalogue.)

Kroutvor, Josef; Setlik, Jiří; and Vlcek, Tomas (eds.). *Moderní český plakát 1918–1945*. Prague: Umělecko Průmyslové Muzeum v Praze, 1984. 56 pp.

Finland

Lainio, Eino (ed.). *Suomalaista käyttögrafiikkaa/ Finnish Graphic Design*. Essays by Hans Björklind, Olof Eriksson, Ahto Numminen, and Jukka Pellinen. Porvoo: Werner Söderström Osakeyhtiö, 1963. 111 pp.

France

Belvès, Pierre. *100 ans d'affiches des chemins de fer*. Paris: 1980. 105 pp.

Capitaine, Jean-Louis, and Charton, Balthazar J. M. *L'affiche de cinéma—le cinéma français*. Paris: Frederic F. Birr, Ateliers H. Labat, 1983. 159 pp.

Davidson, Steef. *Images de la révolte, 1965–1975*. Introduction by Alain Weill. Paris: Musée de l'Affiche et de la Publicité, 1982. 173 pp. (Exhibition catalogue.)

Gaëton-Picon, Geneviève. *Trois siècles d'affiches françaises, 1ᵉ exposition du Musée de l'affiche*. Statements by Robert Bordaz and Jean Casanova. Paris: Musée de l'Affiche, 1978. 84 pp. (Exhibition catalogue.)

Gasquet, Vasco. *Les 500 affiches de mai 68*. Paris: Balland, 1978. 220 pp.

Poitu, Jean-Claude (ed.). *Affiches et luttes syndicales de la CGT*. Preface by Georges Séguy. Paris: Chêne, 1978. 112 pp.

Posters from the Revolution: Paris, May 1986. London: Dobson Books; New York: Bobbs-Merrill, 1969. 96 pp.

Salmon, André. *Maîtres français de l'affiche: Jean Carlu, A. M. Cassandre, Paul Colin, Charles Loupot, Germain Mary*. Paris: Librairie Jose Corti, 1943. 42 pp.

Schardt, Hermann. *Französische Meisterplakate um 1900 aus der Sammlung der Folkwangschule für Gestaltung*. Essen: Folkwangschule für Gestaltung, 1968. 136 pp. (Exhibition catalogue.)

_____. *Paris 1900: Französische Plakatkunst*. Stuttgart: Christian Belser, 1968. 184 pp. 72 plates.

Thon, Christina. *Französische Plakate des 19. Jahrhunderts in der Kunstbibliothek Berlin*. Berlin: Gebr. Mann Verlag, 1968. 43 pp. 32 plates.

Weill, Alain. *Memoire de la rue: Souvenirs d'un imprimeur et d'un afficheur. Archives Karcher: Affiches françaises 1920–1960*. Paris: WM Editions, 1986. 267 pp. (English translation of preface and "A Printer's and Bill Poster's Recollections" laid in. Distributed in the United States by Posters Please, Inc., New York.)

Wichmann, Hans (intro.). *Raymond Savignac: Werke des französischen Plakatkunstlers aus den Jahren 1948 bis heute*. Munich: Die Neue Sammlung, 1982. 49 pp. (Exhibition catalogue.)

Zagrodzki, Christophe (ed.). *L'automobile et la publicité: 100 ans d'automobile française*. Paris: Musée de la Publicité, 1984. 95 pp. (Exhibition catalogue.)

Germany

Arnold, Friedrich (ed.). *Anschläge. Politische Plakate in Deutschland, 1900–1970*. Ebenhausen: Verlag Langewiesche-Brandt, 1972. (166 leaves reproduced in facsimile; 16 pp. of text laid in.)

_____. *Anschläge. 220 politische Plakate als Dokumente der deutschen Geschichte 1900–1980*. Ebenhausen: Verlag Langewiesche-Brandt, 1985. 220 leaves; 20 pp. of text laid in.

Berckenhagen, Ekhart. *Frühe berliner Plakate 1850–1930*. Berlin: Kunstbibliothek, 1963. 43 pp. (Exhibition catalogue.)

Bohrmann, Hans (ed.). *Politische Plakate*. Essays by Ruth Malhotra and Manfred Hagen. Dortmund: Harenberg, 1984. 695 pp. (German political posters, 1870–1983.)

Buddensieg, Tilmann. *Industriekultur: Peter Behrens and the AEG, 1907–1914*. Cambridge, Mass.: MIT Press, 1984. 520 pp.

Cremers, Paul Joseph. *Peter Behrens: Sein Werk von 1909 bis zur Gegenwert*. Essen: Baedeker, 1928. 168 pp.

Festschrift zur Feier des 25jährigen Bestehens der Manoli Zigarettenfabrik zu Berlin. Berlin: Manoli, 1919.

Funk, Anna Christa. *Deutsche Plakate von 1910–1914. Förderung der Plakatkunst durch Karl-Ernst-Osthaus.* Hagen: Karl-Ernst-Osthaus-Museum, 1969. 30 pp. (Exhibition catalogue.)

Herzfelde, Wieland. *John Heartfield: Leben und Werk.* Dresden: VEB Verlag der Kunst, 1976. 3rd ed. 387 pp.

Hillman, Hans, and Rambow, Gunter. *"Ein Plakat ist eine Fläche die ins Auge springt": Plakate der Kasseler Schule.* Frankfurt: Zweitausendeins, 1979. 475 pp.

Medebach, Friedrich. *Das Kampfplakat: Aufgabe, Wesen und Gesetzmässigkeit des politischen Plakats, nachgewiesen an den Plakaten der Kampfjahre von 1918–1933.* Frankfurt am Main: M. Diesterweg, 1941.

Plakate: Gedanke und Kunst, Einiges aus der Plakat-Praxis. Stuttgart: Propaganda Stuttgart, 1912. (64 pp. with 30 lithographed inserts in color.)

Popitz, Klaus. *Plakate der zwanziger Jahre aus der Kunstbibliothek Berlin.* Berlin: Gebr. Mann Verlag, 1977. 119 pp. (8 posters in facsimile folded in pocket.)

Rademacher, Hellmut. *Das deutsche Plakat: Von den Anfängen bis zur Gegenwart.* Dresden: VEB Verlag der Kunst, 1965. 306 pp.

―――. *Deutsche Plakatkunst und ihre Meister.* Leipzig: Edition Leipzig, 1965. 137 pp. (4 posters reproduced in facsimile in accompanying portfolio.)

―――. *Plakatskunst im Klassenkampf, 1924–1932: 24 politische Plakate aus der Zeit der Weimarer Republik 1924–1932.* Leipzig: Zentralantiquariat der DDR, 1974. (Facsimile posters reproduced full size; 12 pp. introduction laid in.)

Schmidt-Linsenhoff, Viktoria; Wettengl, Kurt; Junker, Almut (eds.). *Plakate 1880–1914, Inventarkatalog der Plakatsammlung des Historischen Museums Frankfurt.* Foreword by Reiner Koch. Frankfurt: Historisches Museum Frankfurt, 1986. 485 pp. (Exhibition catalogue.)

Schoch, Reiner (for.). *Politische Plakate der Weimarer Republic 1918–1933.* Essays by Klaus Wolbert, Reiner Diederich, and Richard Grubling. Darmstadt: Hessisches Landesmuseum, 1980. 157 pp. (Exhibition catalogue.)

Weber, Wilhelm. *Peter Behrens, 1869–1940: Gedenkschrift mit Katalog aus Anlass der Ausstellung.* Kaiserslautern: Pfalzgalerie, 1966. (Exhibition catalogue.)

Great Britain

Hutchinson, Harold F. *London Transport Posters.* London: London Transport Board, 1963. 23 pp.; 124 plates.

Picon, Geneviève (intro.). *L'affiche anglaise: Les années 90.* Preface by Roland Barthes; compiled by Laurence Bosse, Anne Kimmel, and Dominique Negel. Paris: Musée des Arts Décoratifs, 1972. 110 pp. (Exhibition catalogue.)

Strong, Ray. *London Transport Posters.* Compiled by Michael Levey. London: Phaidon, 1976. 80 pp.

Italy

Bocca, Giorgio. *I manifesti italiani fra belle epoque e fascismo.* Milan: Fratelli Fabri Editori, 1971. 143 pp.

Il manifesto italiano. Statements by A. M. Brizio and A. Rossi. Milan: Societa per le Belle Arti e Esposizione Permanente, 1965. 55 pp.

Mazzotti, Giuseppe (ed.). *La montagna nei manifesti e nei francobolli de ieri e di oggi.* Treviso: Liberia Editrice Canova, 1967. (Exhibition catalogue.)

Menegazzi, Luigi. *L'epoca d'oro del manifesto: 200 manifesti italiani del 1882 al 1925.* Milan: Electa Editrice, 1977. 138 pp.

Veronesi, Giulia (ed.). *Grafica ricordi "dal manifesto storico all produzione d'avanguardia."* Statements by Sangiorgi and Giorgio Mascherpa. Rome: Ente Premi Roma, 1967. 118 pp. (Exhibition catalogue.)

Japan

L'affiche japonaise: Des origins à nos jours. Statements by Geneviève Gaëton-Picon, Hidemi Kohn, Katsuhiro Yamaguchi, and Yoshiro Imai. Paris: Musée de l'Affiche, 1979. 112 pp. (Exhibition catalogue.)

Calza, Gian Carlo (ed.). *Japanische Plakate Heute: 250 Beispiele von 25 Kunstlern.* Preface by Margit Staber. Milano: Gruppo Editoriale Electa, 1979. 165 pp. (Exhibition catalogue.)

Hara, Hiromu (ed.), for the Tokyo Art Directors' Club. *Nihon no Kokoku Bijutsu—Meijo, Taisho, Showa, 1: Posta (Advertising Art of Japan of the Meiji, Taisho, Showa Eras, v. 1: Posters).* Contributions in Japanese by Masataka Ogawa and Ayao Yamana. Tokyo: Bijutsu Shuppansha, 1967. 270 pp. (Foreword in English and Japanese.)

Kristahn, Heinz-Jürgen, and Mellinghoff, Frieder. *Japanische Plakate: Die Kunst der visuellen Ansprache aus Tradition—In Gegenwart und Zukunft.* Foreword by Makaoto Takahashi. Münsterschwarzach: Vier-Türme-Verlag, 1983. 159 pp.

Stroeve, Ada; de Groot, Elbrig; and Watano, Shigeru (comps.). *Japanese affiches van de laatste 10 jaar.* Amsterdam: Stedelijk Museum, 1977. 28 pp. (Exhibition catalogue.)

Zuan shiryo posta-shu (Design Reference Poster Collection). Compiled by National Postal Museum. Tokyo: Teishin Hakubutsukan, 1937. 124 pp.

The Netherlands

Brattinga, Pieter, Jr., and Dooijes, Dick. *A History of the Dutch Poster, 1890–1966.* Preface by H. L. C. Jaffe. Amsterdam: Scheltema & Holkema, 1968. 170 pp.

Polak, Bettina. *Het Fin-de-siècle in de nederlandse Schilderkunst.* The Hague: Nijhoff, 1955. 415 pp.

Poland

Bojko, Szymon; Czerwinski, Aleksy; and Ksiazek, Zofia (eds.). *Polska sztuka plakatu: Początki k Rozwój do 1939 Roku.* Documentation by Janina Fijalkowska. Warsaw: Wydawnictwo Artystyczno-Graficzne, 1971. 232 pp.

Fijalkowska, Janina. *Muzeum Narodowe w Warszawie. Od młodej polski do naszych dni. Katalog wystawy plakatu (Le développement de l'affiche en Pologne).* Warsaw, 1966. 163 pp. 64 plates. (Text in Polish with French introduction.)

Kowalski, Tadeusz. *Polski Plakat Filmowy.* Warsaw: Filmowa Agencja Wydawnicza, 1957. 142 pp. (Text in Polish, French, Russian, English, and German.)

Mroszczak, Józef (ed.). *Polnische Plakatkunst.* Preface by Jan Lenica; introduction by Jan Białostocki. Vienna: Econ-Verlag, 1962. n.p.

Rutkiewicz, Anna (ed.). *Das polnische Plakat von 1892 bis Heute.* Statements by Heinz-Jürgen Kristahn, Jan Białostocki, Wojciech Makowiecki, Anna Rutkiewicz, Jan Zylinski, and Martin Krampen. Berlin: Hochschule der Künste Berlin, 1980. 192 pp.

Schardt, Hermann. *Vier polnische Plakatkünstler.* (Roman Cieślewicz, Jan Lenica, Józef Mroszczak, Henryk Tomaszewski.) Essen: Deutsches Plakat-Museum, 1971. 38 pp. (Exhibition catalogue.)

Szemberg, Henryk (ed.). *Polish Poster.* Warsaw: Wydawnictwo Artystyczno-Graficzno RSW Prasna, [1957?]. 188 pp.

Wásniewski, Jerzy. *Plakat polski/The Polish Poster.* Edited by Aleksy Czerwinski and Zofia Ksiazek. Warsaw: Wydawnictwo Artystyczno-Graficzno, 1972. 156 pp.

Zanozinski, Jerzy (ed.). *Od Młodej polski do Naszych dni.* Preface by Stanislaw Lorentz; introduction by Janina Fijalkowska. Warsaw: Muzeum Narodowe w Warsawie, 1966. 232 pp. (Introduction in Polish, French, and Russian.)

Spain

L'affiche de guerre/Poster Art in War/El cartell de guerra/El cartel de guerra. Barcelona: Llauger, [1937?]. 44 pp. (Text in French, English, Catalan, and Spanish.)

Sweden

Bjurström, Per. *Svenska reklamaffischer.* Stockholm: Nationalmuseum, 1986. 23 pp. (Exhibition catalogue.)

Lipschutz, Paul (ed.). *Svenska affischer 1895–1979 ur P. Lipschutz Samling.* Stockholm: Kulturhuset, 1979. 33 pp. (Exhibition catalogue.)

Switzerland

Etter, Philipp (intro.). *Das schweizer Plakat/The Swiss Poster/L'affiche suisse/El anuncio suizo/Il cartellone suizzero/O cartaz suiço.* Zurich: Pro Helvetia, 1950. 48 pp. text; 18 pp. plates. (Exhibition catalogue.)

Kulturelle Plakate der Schweiz. Zurich: Kunstgewerbemuseum Zürich, 1974. 80 pp. (Exhibition catalogue.)

Lüthy, Wolfgang (ed.). *Die besten Plakate der Jahre 1941–1965 mit der Ehrenurkunde des eidgenössischen Departementes des Innern.* Preface by Hans Peter Tschudi; essays by Berchtold von Grünigen and Werner Kämpfen. Zurich: Allgemeine Plakatgesellschaft im Verlag der Visualis, 1968. 227 pp. (Text in German, French, and English.)

Margadant, Bruno (ed.). *The Swiss Poster: 1900–1983.* Foreword by Oskar Bätschmann. Basel: Birkhäuser Verlag, 1983. 287 pp. (Text in German, English, and French.)

Meylan, Jean; Maillard, Philippe; and Schenk, Michele. *Bürger zu den Urnen. 75 Jahre eidgenössische Abstimmungen im Spiegel des Plakates.* Lausanne: André Eisele, 1977. 199 pp.

Rotzler, Willy, and Wobmann, Karl. *Political and Social Posters of Switzerland: A Historical Cross-Section.* Zurich: ABC Edition, 1985. 155 pp. (Text in English, German, and French.)

Stutzer, Beat (intro.). *Graubünden im Plakat: Eine kleine Geschichte der Tourismuswerbung von 1890 bis Heute.* Essays by Irma Noseda and Luzi Dosch. Chur: Bündner Kunstmuseum, 1983. 98 pp. (Exhibition catalogue.)

Triet, Max, and Wobmann, Karl (eds.). *Swiss Sport Posters: Historical View of the Best Competition Posters*. Zurich: ABC Verlag, 1983. 151 pp. (Text in English, German, and French.)

Tschanen, Armin, and Bangerter, Walter (eds.). *Official Graphic Art in Switzerland*. Zurich: ABC Verlag, 1964. 184 pp.

Weinberg-Staber, Margit, and Müller, Alois (eds.). *Werbestil 1930–1940. Die alltägliche Bildersprache eines Jahrzehnts*. Zurich: Kunstgewerbemuseum der Stadt Zürich, Museum für Gestaltung, 1981. 180 pp. (Exhibition catalogue.)

Wobmann, Karl (ed.). *Touristikplakate der Schweiz 1880–1940*. Preface by Werner Kämpfen; introduction by Willy Rotzler. Aarau: AT Verlag, 1980. 160 pp. (Text in German, English, French, and Italian.)

Wyder, Bernard (ed.). *Le Valais à l'affiche*. Martigny-Ville: Manoir de Martigny, 1977. 78 pp. (Exhibition catalogue.)

United States

Breitenbach, Edgar, and Cogswell, Margaret. *The American Poster*. New York: The American Federation of Arts and October House, 1967. 71 pp. (Exhibition catalogue.)

Duce, Herbert Cecil. *Poster Advertising*. Chicago: Promotion Bureau of the Poster Advertising Association, 1912. 220 pp.

DeNoon, Christopher (ed.). *Posters of the WPA*. Introduction by Francis V. O'Connor; essays by Anthony Velonis, Jim Heimann, and Richard Floethe. Los Angeles: The Wheatley Press in association with the University of Washington Press, Seattle, 1987. 175 pp.

Garrigan, John (intro.). *Images of an Era: The American Poster 1945–1975*. Essays by Margaret Cogswell, Milton Glaser, Dore Ashton, and Alan Gowans. Washington, D.C.: Smithsonian Institution, 1975. 20 pp. text; 257 plates.

Johnson, J. Stewart. *The Modern American Poster*. New York: The Museum of Modern Art, 1984. 180 pp. (Exhibition catalogue.)

Kiehl, David W. *American Art Posters of the 1890s in The Metropolitan Museum of Art, Including The Leonard A. Lauder Collection*. Essays by Kiehl, Phillip Dennis Cate, and Nancy Finlay. New York: The Metropolitan Museum of Art, 1987. 199 pp.

Kunzle, David (ed.). *American Posters of Protest 1966–1970*. Foreword by Paul Mocsanyi. New York: New School Art Center, 1971. 81 pp. (Exhibition catalogue.)

List, Vera, and Kupferberg, Herbert. *Lincoln Center Posters*. New York: Harry N. Abrams, 1980. 63 pp.

Medeiros, Walter. *San Francisco Rock Poster Art*. Preface by Henry Hopkins. San Francisco: San Francisco Museum of Modern Art, 1976. 32 pp. (Exhibition catalogue.)

New York Art on the Road: A Collection of Posters from Exhibitions Organized by New York State Cultural Institutions and Circulated Nationwide. Statements by Hugh L. Carey, Kitty Hart, and George Weissman. New York: Cultural Affairs Department, Philip Morris Incorporated, 1980. 32 pp. (Exhibition catalogue.)

Schmidt, Werner (ed.). *Kunstlerplakate aus den USA: Graphische Blätter und Zeichnungen aus dem Dresdner Kupferstich-Kabinett*. Dresden: Staatliche Kunstsammlungen Dresden, Kupferstich-Kabinett, 1980. 79 pp. (Exhibition catalogue.)

USSR

Baburina, Nina I. *Russkii Plakat vtoroi poloviny XIX–nachala XX veka*. Moscow: Khudozhnik RSFSR, 1983.

———. *Sowjetische Stummfilmplakate*. Forewords by Jürgen Harten and Klaus Schrenk. Düsseldorf: Städtische Kunsthalle, 1985. 36 pp. (Exhibition catalogue.)

Bojko, Szymon. *New Graphic Design in Revolutionary Russia*. Preface by Herbert Spencer. New York: Praeger Publishers, 1972. 156 pp.

Constantine, Mildred, and Fern, Alan M. *Revolutionary Soviet Film Posters*. Baltimore and London: The Johns Hopkins University Press, 1974. 97 pp.

Duvakin, V. D. *ROSTA Fenster, Majakowski als Dichter und Bildender Künstler*. Dresden: VEB Verlag der Kunst, 1975. 237 pp.

Lebedev, I. V. V., and Punin, N. N. *Russkii Plakat 1917–1922*. Petersburg: "Strelets," 1922. 36 pp.

Liakhov, Volia Nikolavich (comp.). *Sovetskii reklamnyi plakat 1917–1932*. Edited by V. Pankratova. Moscow: Sovetskii Khudozhnik, 1972. 127 pp.

Plitz, Georg. *Russland wird rot: Satirische Plakate 1918–1922*. East Berlin: Eulenspiegel Verlag, 1977. 127 pp.

Polonskii, V. P. *Russkii revolyutsionnyi plakat*. Moscow: Gosizdat, 1925. 192 pp.

Russian Revolutionary Posters, 1917–1927. Statements by Caio Garruba and Stefan Congrat-Butlar. New York: Grove Press, 1967. 16 pp. 40 plates.

INDIVIDUAL DESIGNERS

Jean Arp

Arntz, Wilhelm F. *Hans (Jean) Arp. Das graphische Werk 1912–1966/L'oeuvre gravé/The Graphic Work*. The Hague/Oberbayern: Verlag Gertrud Arntz-Winter, 1980.

Otto Baumberger

Baumberger, Otto. *Blick nach Aussen und Innen*. Weiningen-Zurich, 1966.

Rotzler, Willy. *Otto Baumberger: Ein Pionier der schweizer Plakatkunst*. Bern: Plakatgalerie Klubschule, 1983.

Herbert Bayer

Cohen, Arthur. *Herbert Bayer: The Complete Work*. Cambridge, Mass.: MIT Press, 1984.

Hahn, Peter. *Herbert Bayer: Das druckgraphische Werk bis 1971*. Berlin: Bauhaus Archiv, 1974.

Aubrey Beardsley

Reade, Brian. *Aubrey Beardsley*. Introduction by John Rothenstein. New York: Viking Press; London: Studio Vista, Ltd., 1967. 372 pp.

Weintraub, Stanley. *Aubrey Beardsley: Imp of the Perverse*. College Park, Penn.: Pennsylvania State University Press, 1976.

The Beggarstaffs: William Nicholson and James Pryde

Hudson, Derek. *James Pryde, 1866–1941*. London: Constable, 1949. 99 pp.

Steen, Marguerite. *William Nicholson*. London: Collins, 1943. 229 pp.

Max Bill

Max Bill: Das druckgraphische Werk bis 1968. Nuremburg: Kunsthalle Albrecht Dürer-Gesellschaft, 1968. (Exhibition catalogue.)

Pierre Bonnard

Roger-Marx, Claude. *Bonnard lithographe*. Monte Carlo: Andre Sauret Editions du Livre, 1952.

Will Bradley

Will Bradley: His Chap Book. New York: The Typophiles, 1955. 104 pp.

Alexey Brodovitch

Alexey Brodovitch and His Influence: Exhibition and Catalog. Philadelphia: Philadelphia College of Art, 1972. 48 pp.

Porter, Allen, and Tourdjman, Georges. *Alexey Brodovitch*. Paris: Grand Palais, 1982. 139 pp. (Exhibition catalogue.)

Max Burchartz

Max Burchartz. Essen: Folkwangschule, 1961. (Exhibition catalogue.)

Fritz Bühler

von Grünigen, Berchtold; Steiner, Heiri; and Staehelin, Walter. *Gedächtnisausstellung Fritz Bühler/Pierre Gauchat*. Basel: Gewerbemuseum Basel, 1964.

Emile Cardinaux

Bolt, Thomas (ed.). *Emile Cardinaux (1877–1936)*. Foreword by Hansjörg Budliger. Zurich: Kunstgewerbemuseum, 1985. 48 pp. (Exhibition catalogue.)

Jean Carlu

Weill, Alain (ed.). *Retrospective Jean Carlu*. Foreword by Geneviève Gaëtan-Picon. Paris: Musée de l'Affiche, 1980. 62 pp. (Exhibition catalogue.)

A. M. Cassandre

Brown, Robert K., and Reinhold, Susan. *The Poster Art of A. M. Cassandre*. New York: E. P. Dutton, 1979. 89 pp.

Fantl, E. M. *Posters by Cassandre*. New York: The Museum of Modern Art, 1936. 16 pp. (Exhibition catalogue.)

Mouron, Henri. *A. M. Cassandre*. New York: Rizzoli, 1985. 315 pp.

Jules Chéret

Broido, Lucy. *Posters of Jules Chéret: 46 Full-Color Plates and an Illustrated Catalogue Raisonné*. New York: Dover, 1980. 128 pp.

Seymour Chwast

Seymour Chwast. Tokyo: Seibundo Shinkosha, 1973.

The Left-Handed Designer. Interview: Seymour Chwast and Steven Heller. New York: Harry N. Abrams, 1985. 143 pp.

Roman Cieślewicz

Bailly, Jean-Christophe (ed.). *Plakate, Affiches, Posters*. Foreword by Dorit Marhenke; introduction by Karl Dedecius. Heidelberg: Braus, 1984. 148

pp. (Exhibition catalogue; text in English, French, and German.)

Robert Delaunay

Vriesen, Gustav, and Imdahl, Max. *Robert Delaunay: Light and Color.* New York: Harry N. Abrams, 1969.

Walter Dexel

Vitt, Walter. *Walter Dexel: Werkverzeichnis der Druckgraphik von 1915 bis 1971.* Cologne: Buchhandlung Walther König, 1971.

Theo van Doesburg

Baljeu, Joost. *Theo van Doesburg.* London: Studio Vista, 1974.

James Ensor

Taevernier, Auguste. *James Ensor: Catalogue illustré de ses gravures, leur déscription critique et l'inventaire des plaques.* Brussels: Mme Paul van der Perre, 1973.

Hans Erni

Cailler, Pierre. *Catalogue raisonné de l'oeuvre lithographié et gravé de Hans Erni. Tome 1, 1930 à 1957.* Geneva: Editions Pierre Cailler, 1959.

————. *Catalogue raisonné de l'oeuvre lithographié et gravé de Hans Erni. Tome 2, 1958 à 1970.* Geneva: Editions Pierre Cailler, 1971.

Rotzler, Willy. *Hans Erni: Plakate 1929–1976.* Lucerne: Verlag Kunstkreis, 1976.

Max Ernst

Spies, Werner (ed.). *Max Ernst: Oeuvre-Katalog 1, Das Graphischewerk.* Cologne: Dumont, 1975.

Akseli Gallen-Kallela

Okkonen, Onni. *Akseli Gallen-Kallelan Taidetta.* Porvoosa, 1948.

Pierre Gauchat

Fischli, Hans, and Steiner, Heiri. *Pierre Gauchat: Der Grafiker.* Zurich: Kunstgewerbemuseum, 1960.

Winfred Gaul

Freitag, Eberhard. *Werk ver Zeichnis der Druckgraphiken und Objekte.* Kiel: Kunsthalle und Schleswig-Holsteinischer Kunstverein, 1978.

Milton Glaser

Glaser, Milton. *Milton Glaser, Graphic Design.* Woodstock, N.Y.: Overlook Press, 1973. 242 pp.

Soavi, Giorgio. *The Milton Glaser Poster Book.* New York: Harmony Books, 1977. 47 pp.

Grapus

Weill, Alain. *Grapus.* Paris: Musée de l'Affiche et de la Publicité, [1982?]. 119 pp. (Exhibition catalogue.)

Hector Guimard

Graham, F. Lanier. *Hector Guimard.* New York: The Museum of Modern Art, 1970. 36 pp.

Ferdinand Hodler

Ferdinand Hodler und das schweizer Künstlerplakat. Zurich: Kunstgewerbemuseum Zürich, 1983. 155 pp. (Exhibition catalogue.)

Ludwig Hohlwein

Duvigneau, Volker. *Ludwig Hohlwein (1874–1949). Ein Meister deutscher Plakatkunst.* Munich: Stadtmuseum, 1970. (Exhibition catalogue.)

Frenzel, Hermann K. (ed.). *Ludwig Hohlwein.* Foreword by Walter F. Schubert. Berlin: Phönix, 1926. 71 pp. (Text in German and English.)

Schneegass, Christian (ed.). *Ludwig Hohlwein: Plakate der Jahre 1906–1940 aus der Graphischen Sammlung Staatsgalerie Stuttgart.* Essen: Deutsches Plakatmuseum, 1985. 135 pp. (Exhibition catalogue.)

Max Huber

Huber, Max; Pirovano, Carlo; and Gardini, Christina (eds.). *Max Huber: Progetti grafici 1936–1981.* Milan: Gruppo Editoriale Electa, 1982. 118 pp.

Yusaku Kamekura

Ogawa, Masatka; Tanaka, Ikko; and Nagai, Kazumasa. *The Works of Yusaku Kamekura.* Tokyo: Rikuyoi-sha Publishing, 1983. 267 pp.

E. McKnight Kauffer

Havinden, Ashley. *Memorial Exhibition of the Work of E. McKnight Kauffer.* Statements by Francis Meynell and Thomas Eckersley. London: Victoria and Albert Museum, 1955. (Exhibition catalogue.)

Haworth-Booth, Mark. *E. McKnight Kauffer: A Designer and His Public.* London: Gordon Fraser, 1979. 136 pp.

Posters by E. McKnight Kauffer. Foreword by Aldous Huxley; statement by Kauffer. New York: The Museum of Modern Art, 1937. 24 pp.

Ernst Keller

Ernst Keller: Graphiker 1891–1968 Gesamtwerk. Zurich: Kunstgewerbemuseum, 1976.

Gustav Klutsis

Oginskaia, L. *Gustav Klutsis.* Sovetskii Khudozhnik, 1981. 200 pp.

Oskar Kokoschka

Wingler, Hans, and Welz, Friedrich. *Oskar Kokoschka: Das druckgraphische Werk.* Salzburg: Verlag Galerie Welz, 1975.

————. *Oskar Kokoschka: Das druckgraphische Werk II, Druckgraphik 1975–1980.* Salzburg: Verlag Galerie Welz, 1981.

Takashi Kono

Ito, Itsuhei. *Takashi Kono—Designer.* Tokyo: Nishikawa Book Store, 1956. 88 pp. (Captions and text partly in English.)

Kono, Takashi. *My Momentum.* Tokyo: Rikuyoi-Sha Publishing, 1983. 190 pp. (Text in English and Japanese.)

Jan Lenica

Gorschenek, Margareta; Kristahn, Heinz-Jürgen; and Rucktäschel, Annamaria (eds.). *Jan Lenica Plakat- und Filmkunst.* Berlin: Frölich und Kaufmann, 1981. 190 pp.

Leo Lionni

Leo Lionni: Plastiken, Ölbilder, Zeichnungen, Druckgraphik. Cologne, 1974. (Exhibition catalogue.)

El Lissitzky

Küppers-Lissitzky, Sophie. *El Lissitzky: Life, Let-* *ters, Texts.* Greenwich, Conn.: New York Graphic Society Ltd., 1968. 407 pp. (Translation of *El Lissitzky: Maler, Architekt, Typograf, Fotograf.* Dresden: VEB Verlag der Kunst, 1967.)

Bertold Löffler

Bertold Löffler. Vienna: Osterreichisches Museum für angewandte Kunst, 1978. (Exhibition catalogue.)

Bertold Löffler. Vienna: Galerie Metropol, 1980. (Exhibition catalogue.)

Charles Loupot

Weill, Alain (intro.). *Charles Loupot.* Foreword by Geneviève Gaëtan-Picon. Paris: Musée de l'Affiche, 1979. 62 pp. (Exhibition catalogue.)

Charles Rennie Mackintosh

Howarth, Thomas. *Charles Rennie Mackintosh and the Modern Movement.* London: Routledge and Kegen Paul; New York: Wittenborn, 1953. 357 pp.

Man Ray

Anselmino, L. *Man Ray, opera grafica.* Turin, 1973.

Penrose, Roland. *Man Ray.* London: Thames & Hudson, 1975. 208 pp.

Herbert Matter

Herbert Matter: A Retrospective. Introduction by Paul Rand. New Haven, Conn.: Yale University, School of Art, 1978. 32 pp. (Exhibition catalogue.)

Peter Max

Peter Max Superposter Book. New York: Crown Publishers, 1971. 38 pp.

Johannes Molzahn

Salzmann, Siegfried, and Güse, E.-G. *Johannes Molzahn: Das druckgraphische Werk.* Duisburg: Wilhelm-Lehmbruck-Museum, 1977.

Otto Morach

Schaller, Marie Louise. *Die Geschichte eines Plakates: Otto Morach, ein Plakatgestalter der zwanziger Jahre.* Zurich: J. E. Wolfensberger AG, 1980.

Koloman Moser

Fenz, Werner. *Koloman Moser: Graphik, Kunstgewerbe, Malerei.* Vienna: Residenz Verlag, 1984. 264 pp.

Alphonse Mucha

Alfons Mucha 1860–1939. Contributions by Bernd Krimmel, Jiří Kotalík, Jana Brabcová, Geneviève Lacambre, and Marc Bascou. Darmstadt: Mathildenhöhe, 1980. 419 pp.

Mucha, Jiří. *Alphonse Mucha: His Life and Art.* London: Heinemann, 1966; Prague: Artia Verlag, 1965. 391 pp.

Rennert, Jack, and Weill, Alain. *Alphonse Mucha: The Complete Posters and Panels.* Boston: G. K. Hall, 1984. 405 pp.

Bruno Munari

Meneguzzo, Marco, and Quirico, Tiziana (eds.). *Bruno Munari.* Milan: Edizioni Electa, 1986. 107 pp.

Joseph Maria Olbrich

Latham, Ian. *Joseph Maria Olbrich.* New York: Rizzoli, 1980. 156 pp.

Eduardo Paolozzi

Miles, Rosemary. *The Complete Prints of Eduardo Paolozzi*. London: Victoria and Albert Museum, 1977.

Edward Penfield

Gibson, David. *Designed to Persuade: The Graphic Art of Edward Penfield*. Yonkers, N.Y.: Hudson River Museum, 1984. 33 pp. (Exhibition catalogue.)

Hans Poelzig

Heuss, Theodor. *Hans Poelzig: Bauten und Entwurfe*. Berlin, 1939.

Posener, Julius (ed.). Hans Poelzig: *Gesammelteschriften und Werke*. Berlin, 1970.

Jan Preisler

Matíček, Antonín. *Jan Preisler*. Prague: Melantrich, 1950. 118 pp. 257 plates.

Jan Preisler 1872–1918. Prague: Narodni Galerie v Praze, 1964.

Paul Rand

Kamekura, Yusaku (ed.). *Paul Rand: His Work from 1946 to 1958*. New York: Alfred A. Knopf; Tokyo: Zokeisha, 1959. 132 pp. (Text in English and Japanese.)

Rand, Paul. *A Designer's Art*. New Haven: Yale University Press, 1985. 239 pp.

———. *Thoughts on Design*. New York: Wittenborn, Schultz, Inc., 1947. 159 pp. (Text in English, French, and Spanish.)

Alexander Rodchenko

Khan-Magomedov, Selim. *Rodchenko: The Complete Work*. Boston: MIT Press, 1986. 275 pp.

Xanti Schawinsky

Holz, Hans Heinz. *Xanti Schawinsky: Bewegung im Raum*. Zurich: ABC Verlag, 1981. 139 pp.

Paul, Barbara (ed.). *Xanti Schawinski: Malerei, Bühne, Grafikdesign, Fotografie*. Berlin: Bauhaus Archiv, 1986. 221 pp.

Egon Schiele

Kallir, Otto. *Egon Schiele: Das druckgraphische Werk*. Vienna: Paul Zsolnay Verlag, 1970. (Text in German and English.)

Oskar Schlemmer

Grohmann, Will, and Schlemmer, Tut. *Oskar Schlemmer: Zeichnungen und Graphik, Oeuvre-Katalog*. Stuttgart: Verlag Gerd Hatje, 1965.

Joost Schmidt

Loew, Heinz, and Nonne-Schmidt, Helene. *Joost Schmidt: Lehre und Arbeit am Bauhaus 1919–1932*. Düsseldorf: Edition Marzona, 1984. 118 pp.

Paul Schuitema

Buchmann, Mark (ed.). *Ein Pionier der holländischen Avantgarde, Paul Schuitema*. Zurich: Kunstgewerbemuseum, 1967. 8 pp. (Exhibition catalogue.)

Kurt Schwitters

Elderfield, John. *Kurt Schwitters*. London: Thames and Hudson, 1985. 424 pp.

Ben Shahn

Prescott, Kenneth W. *The Complete Graphic Works of Ben Shahn*. New York: The New York Times Book Co., 1973.

Soby, James Thrall. *Ben Shahn: His Graphic Art*. New York: George Braziller, 1957. 139 pp.

Stahl-Arpke

Hohenstein, Siglinde (ed.). *Otto Arpke (1886–1943): Werk und Wirkung*. Mainz: Gutenberg Museum, 1981. 62 pp. (Exhibition catalogue.)

Franciszek Starowieyski

Coates, Robert. *Posters by Franciszek Starowieyski*. Statement by Starowieyski. New York: The Museum of Modern Art, 1985. 15 pp. (Exhibition catalogue.)

Vladimir and Georgii Stenberg

Monumental'noe iskusstvo: Stenbergovskii stil'. Teatr. Plakat. Introductions by Nina Ivanovna Baburina and Alla Mikhailovna Zaitseva; compiled by Baburina and Galina Vasil'evna Maricheva. Moscow: Moskovskaia organizatsilia Soiuza khudozhnikov RSFSR, 1984. 62 pp. (Exhibition catalogue with detailed chronology; text in Russian.)

Niklaus Stoecklin

Hartmann, Hans, and Budliger, Hansjörg (eds.). *Niklaus Stoecklin 1896–1982*. Foreword by Frieder Mellinghoff; statements by Bruno Haldner, Hans Hartmann, and Stefan Paradowski. Basel: Gewerbemuseum Basel, Museum für Gestaltung, 1986. 98 pp. (Exhibition catalogue.)

Ikko Tanaka

Tanaka Ikko no dezain/The Work of Ikko Tanaka. Kyoto: Shinshindo, 1975. 215 pp. (Text in English and Japanese.)

Johan Thorn-Prikker

Wember, Paul. *Johan Thorn-Prikker, Glasfenster, Wandbilder, Ornamente 1891–1932*. Catalogue by Johannes Cladders. Krefeld: Scherpe Verlag, 1966. 260 pp.

Jan Toorop

De Grafiek van Jan Toorop. Amsterdam: Rijksprentenkabinet/Rijksmuseum, 1969.

Henri de Toulouse-Lautrec

Castleman, Riva, and Wittrock, Wolfgang (eds.). *Henri de Toulouse-Lautrec: Images of the 1890s*. Introduction by Castleman; essays by Julia Frey, Matthias Arnold, and Phillip Dennis Cate; catalogue by Wittrock. New York: The Museum of Modern Art, 1985. 262 pp. (Exhibition catalogue.)

Julien, Edouard. *The Posters of Toulouse-Lautrec*. Boston: Boston Book & Art Shop, 1966. 97 pp.

Wittrock, Wolfgang. *Toulouse-Lautrec: The Complete Prints*. London: Sotheby's Publications, 1985. 2 vols. 831 pp. (Translated and edited by Catherine E. Kuehn.)

Niklaus Troxler

Rotzler, Willy. *Niklaus Troxler*. Bern: Plakatgalerie Klubschule, 1981.

Jan Tschichold

McLean, Ruari. *Jan Tschichold: Typographer*. Boston: David Godine, 1975. 160 pp.

Andy Warhol

Wünsche, Hermann. *Andy Warhol: Das graphische Werk 1962–1980*. Königswinter am Rhein: Galerie Vorburg, 1981.

Tadanori Yokoo

Posters for Music by Tadanori Yokoo. Nishiwaki: Okanoyama Museum of Art, 1986. 62 pp. (Exhibition catalogue.)

Tadanori Yokoo in Kobe. Nishiwaki: Okanoyama Museum of Art, 1985. 74 pp. (Exhibition catalogue.)

Ilia Zdanevitch

Isselbacher, Audrey (ed.). *Iliazd and the Illustrated Book*. Essays by Isselbacher and Françoise Le Gris-Bergmann. New York: The Museum of Modern Art, 1987. 88 pp. (Exhibition catalogue.)

Piet Zwart

Müller, Fridolin (ed.). *Piet Zwart*. New York: Hastings House, 1966. 112 pp. (Text in German, English, and French.)

PERIODICALS

Affiches (Tokyo), 1923–1932(?)

Die besten Plakate des Jahres (Basel), 1942 to date. Annual publication of the Swiss Department of the Interior showing posters selected for this honor. Published in German and French since its inception. In 1976 title was changed to *Schweizer Plakate*.

Bienále Brno. Mezinárodní výstava propagacŃi grafiky a plakátu (Brno), 1974 to date.

Biennale plakatu Warszawa (Warsaw), 1966 to date. Text in Polish and English.

Graphis Posters (Zurich), 1973 to date.

Die hundert besten Plakate des Jahres (East Berlin), 1983 to date?

International Poster Annual (St. Gall), 1948/49–1972.

Lahti Poster Biennale (Lahti), 1973 to date. Text in Finnish and English.

Modern Publicity (London), 1924 to date. (From 1924 as *Posters and Their Designers*; from 1925 as *Art and Publicity*; from 1926 to 1930 as *Posters and Publicity*.)

Das Plakat (Berlin), 1913–1921. (From 1910 to 1912 as *Mitteilungen des Vereins der Plakatfreunde*.)

Poster (Chicago), 1910–1930.

Poster and Art Collector (London), 1898–1901.

Poster Collector's Circular (London), 1899.

Poster Lore (Kansas City, Mo.), 1896.

Prämierte Plakate (Zurich and Basel), 1941 to date. Annual publication of posters awarded prizes by the Swiss Department of the Interior. Published by the Allgemeine Plakatgesellschaft. Published in French, Italian, and English in addition to German since 1982.

Projekt (Warsaw), 1956 to date.

PS: The Journal of the Poster Society (New York), 1986 to date.

INDEX OF ILLUSTRATIONS

This listing of illustrations is organized alphabetically by the name of the designer. Works for which the designer is unknown appear at the end of the listing. Figure numbers are given for black-and-white illustrations. Plate numbers in italics indicate color illustrations.